Power in Practice

Power in Practice

Clergy Workplace Experiences Within the
Pentecostal Assemblies of Canada

RYAN MORGAN

☙PICKWICK *Publications* • Eugene, Oregon

POWER IN PRACTICE
Clergy Workplace Experiences Within the Pentecostal Assemblies of Canada

Copyright © 2025 Ryan Morgan. All rights reserved. Except for brief quotations in critical publications or reviews, no part of this book may be reproduced in any manner without prior written permission from the publisher. Write: Permissions, Wipf and Stock Publishers, 199 W. 8th Ave., Suite 3, Eugene, OR 97401.

Pickwick Publications
An Imprint of Wipf and Stock Publishers
199 W. 8th Ave., Suite 3
Eugene, OR 97401

www.wipfandstock.com

PAPERBACK ISBN: 979-8-3852-4353-2
HARDCOVER ISBN: 979-8-3852-4354-9
EBOOK ISBN: 979-8-3852-4355-6

Cataloguing-in-Publication data:

Names: Morgan, Ryan [author].

Title: Power in practice : cergy workplace experiences within the Pentecostal Assemblies of Canada / Ryan Morgan.

Description: Eugene, OR: Pickwick Publications, 2025. Includes bibliographical references and index.

Identifiers: ISBN 979-8-3852-4353-2 (paperback) | ISBN 979-8-3852-4354-9 (hardcover) | ISBN 979-8-3852-4355-6 (ebook)

Subjects: LCSH: Power (Christian theology). | Clergy—Professional ethics. | Abuse of administrative power—Religious aspects—Christianity. | Pentecostal Assemblies of Canada—Clergy. | Clergy—Abuse of.

Classification: BV4398 M674 2025 (paperback) | BV4398 (ebook)

07/14/25

This dissertation was supervised at London School of Theology and submitted to Middlesex University as per requirement for the degree of Master of Theology (MTh) in March 2024.

It was examined by Dr. Peter Althouse (external examiner), Dr. Alistair McKitterick (internal examiner), and Dr. Jean-Marc Heimerdinger (independent chair) and approved in June 2024.

All Scripture quotations, unless otherwise indicated, are taken from the Holy Bible, New International Version®, NIV®. Copyright © 2011 by Biblica, Inc.™ Used by permission of Zondervan. All rights reserved worldwide. www.zondervan.com. The "NIV" and "New International Version" are trademarks registered in the United States Patent and Trademark Office by Biblica, Inc.™

Contents

Acknowledgments | vii
Dedication | ix
Disclaimer: Interview Confidentiality and Citations | xiii
List of Abbreviations | xv

1   Introduction | 1
     Purpose of this Study | 1
     Methodology | 2
     Interview Method and Results | 15
     Context and Background | 16

2   Findings | 21
     Chapter Overview | 21
     An Autopsy of Declining Clergy Retention | 23
     Indifference | 33
     Inequality | 45
     Indignity | 55
     A Special Note on Illegal Behaviour | 70
     Chapter Conclusion | 74

Contents

3 Literature Review | 76
   A Note on the Absence of Specific Literature | 76
   A Philosophy and Theology of Power for the Church | 77
   Theological Anthropology and Vocation | 81
   The Abuse of Power within the Church | 83

4 Theological Response | 96
   Chapter Overview | 96
   Rightly Bearing God's Name | 97
   Imago Dei | 100
   Submission and Abuse | 113
   The Renewed Praxis | 117

5 Conclusion and Recommendations | 121
   Chapter Overview | 121
   Recommended Practices for the PAOC | 122
   The Challenge of Narcissism | 130
   An Attitude of Grace | 137
   Research Conclusion | 140

Bibliography | 141

Acknowledgments

THE RELATIVELY SHORT ROAD of this research programme was unexpectedly lengthened several times by the sort of health emergencies that are too big, and too scary, to speak briefly about. To that end, I would like to express my most sincere appreciation to my supervisors, Mark Cartledge and Christopher Steed, for their kindness and patient support as I pressed onward.

But most especially, to my dear wife Amber, who cared for our children, the responsibilities of our household, and her exhausted husband . . . *thank you*. I would have given up long ago if you weren't so good at believing in me. This project would have been impossible without you.

Kyleigh, Maycie, AJ, Mom and Dad: Thank you for your generosity toward me (especially the sacrifice of time) so I could complete this work.

Dedication

ON MAY 19, 2023, the FX network aired the first of four parts in a documentary about Hillsong, the church/record label/event company that had become a global religious enterprise. Featuring the investigative reporting of *Vanity Fair* journalists David Adler and Alex French, this exposé of the embattled megachurch highlighted a long-term culture of abuse, exploitation, and image management.[1] Ultimately, the documentary concluded that the power dynamics among the senior leadership at Hillsong led directly to unethical (and allegedly illegal) behaviour. This kind of revelation, of course, begs the significant question of the present ecclesial era: How could such toxicity be perpetuated for decades while worshippers looked on?[2] Former (and fired) Hillsong pastor Carl Lentz might have provided one of the answers:[3] "Why is it hard for people to speak out against Hillsong Church? Because they've signed NDAs, that's why."[4]

Controlling speech (and in particular, the attempt to control the speech of current and former clergy) became a tool that, when

---

1. Jones, "Hulu Series Shows the Gravity."
2. Perhaps the same question that the collapses of Mars Hill Church (*Christianity Today*, "Who Killed Mars Hill?") and Willow Creek Church also prompt (Beaty, *Celebrities for Jesus*, 58). The familiarity of this discussion is as disheartening as the subject itself.
3. Taylor, "Carl Lentz Is Fired."
4. *Secrets of Hillsong*, "False Prophets."

Dedication

used, directly eroded the health and integrity of this institution. A lack of accountability and the allure of expediency ultimately created an environment where abuses multiplied; cover-ups (and the associated passivity they facilitated) were simply accepted as a necessary reality for those engaged in a twenty-first-century Christian mission.

It was not until my data collection was complete that I saw *The Secrets of Hillsong*, yet I could scarcely believe the parallels between several of the stories director Stacey Lee brought to the screen and the stories I had heard over the course of my interviews with PAOC pastors. While both the particulars of the history of Hillsong and its sheer scale are unique, the overall themes and dynamics presented in the four-part series were strikingly consistent with what I had heard and observed throughout this project.

There is a holy discomfort that surfaces in the face of these sorts of revelations; for me, this led to a long look at the movement that nurtured my faith in Christ as a child and provided a community to be "my people." It is difficult to hold the tension between the service I attended last Sunday in a PAOC church (which was so full of truth and spiritual vibrancy) and the unexpected stories of devastation that I catalogued for this project (and have also myself experienced).

In seminary, I learned that Paul's word of choice for the ongoing sanctification of the church in Eph 4:12 is καταρτισμός (*katartismos*). As my professor suggested, perhaps the translations that render this word as "equip" are painting too serene a picture. Whether broken bones or broken nets, καταρτισμός is the work of mending: broken, fractured, torn up . . . but being put back together by Christ.[5] That is the mending that must take place; in each believer, but especially now in the body of clergy who are also entrusted with the ministry of καταρτισμός themselves.

With this awareness, it is to the broken, fractured, torn-up, and subsequently silenced clergy whom I dedicate this work. My prayer has been that in the undertaking of this project I might,

---

5. I am greatly indebted to the late Eugene Peterson, professor emeritus of spiritual theology at Regent College (Vancouver), for this insight.

Dedication

in some small way, participate in both the καταρτισμός of Christian ethics within my church family and the καταρτισμός of hope within the body of our clergy. May grace and truth bring this kind of restoration and renewal, and as the psalmist declares, may the Lord himself tend to your precious wounds (Ps 137:3).

Disclaimer: Interview Confidentiality and Citations

THE INTERVIEWS CONDUCTED FOR this study are confidential, and as such the citation of interview transcripts and associated field notes omit the names of the interviewee, as per the confidentiality terms in the research consent form.

Further, as the interviews were conducted via video conference, the specific dates of each interview are withheld due to the multiple means by which participant and network computer logs, account records, and digital calendars could correlate these dates to a specific identity. As noted in chapter 1, appropriate pseudonyms are used instead of participant names, and identifying details in their story (geography, names of individuals, etc.) have been redacted.

As such, citations related to the research interviews include only an interview code, such as "S1P1." To clarify the specific source, citations will specify either "interview transcript" or "field notes" (e.g., interview transcript S2P4; field notes S3P2). In the case where the interview subject is clearly identified with a pseudonym, the interview code is dropped altogether in the footnote (e.g., interview transcript).

All participant data was destroyed after having satisfied the examiners for this study, as per the terms of the research consent form.

List of Abbreviations

ABNWT	Alberta and Northwest Territory District of the PAOC
BCYD	BC and Yukon District of the PAOC
DE	District executive
DLT	District leadership team
ESA	Employment Standards Act
EOND	Eastern Ontario and Nunavut District of the PAOC
HR	Human resources
NDA	Nondisclosure agreement
NICNT	New International Commentary on the New Testament
NPD	Narcissistic personality disorder
$NPNF^2$	*Nicene and Post-Nicene Fathers*, 2nd ser.
PAOC	Pentecostal Assemblies of Canada
ROE	Record of employment
SOET	"Statement of Essential Truths and Positions and Practices." PAOC, May 2022. https://my.paoc.org/church/files/statement-of-essential-truths-and-positions-and-practices_june2022.pdf

LIST OF ABBREVIATIONS

SOFET	"Statement of Fundamental and Essential Truths." PAOC, 2014. https://paoc.org/docs/default-source/fellowship-services-documents/statement-of-fundamental-and-essential-truths.pdf?sfvrsn=153a1d6a_0
TAR	Theological action research
VTSup	Supplements to Vetus Testamentum
WOD	Western Ontario District of the PAOC

1

Introduction

PURPOSE OF THIS STUDY

THE PURPOSE OF THIS study is to examine the experiences of a diverse group of current and former clergy affiliated with the Pentecostal Assemblies of Canada (PAOC), within professional contexts marked by internal power differentials. This research is conducted to better understand the formal and informal structures of power and authority in the PAOC, their impact on members of the clergy, and to reflect upon the theological perspectives of the denomination in regard to the same.[1] The research question is as follows:

---

1. As noted by the PAOC general superintendent, "Historically, we have resisted the word *denomination*, as for many it speaks of institutionalization and inflexible structures and tradition. While aspects of these concerns are certainly valid and are continually addressed, we do know that the external world—Christian, religious, and secular—views us as a Christian Protestant denomination within the Pentecostal and charismatic streams. For those reasons and for legal purposes, denomination is an accurate word" (Wells, "What We Call Ourselves," para. 2).

While this study will prefer the term *denomination* for clarity, when the term *fellowship* appears (especially within the internal documents of the PAOC), it should not be interpreted as "people collectively with whom a person habitually socializes or associates" but rather as the specific "spiritual communication or religious communion" (*Oxford English Dictionary*, s.v. "Fellowship"), composed of both the clergy and congregants who comprise the whole of the PAOC.

"What are the experiences of PAOC credential holders in regard to their relationships with other credential holders on the subject of power and position?" This is an intentionally open-ended inquiry that does not presume the abuse of power but rather sets out to draw insights from the descriptions provided by participants regarding their own experiences. The goal of this inquiry is to collect data that might be useful in identifying both espoused and operant theologies at work within the ecclesial system for comparison to the formal and normative voices of theology. In doing so, this study seeks to construct an account which is accurately descriptive of the current praxis of the denomination, while also providing a prescriptive framework for a theologically informed transformation stemming from rigorous critique.

METHODOLOGY

Location Within the Disciplines

The need to think theologically about qualitative data, as well as the broad practices of Christian faith, led to the development of this project as an exercise in practical theology. Assuming interdisciplinarity, practical theology is especially concerned with accurately articulating the reality of a particular situation, while also reflecting on significant "connections between theology and faith practice, and between the Christian tradition and the present,"[2] making it the ideal discipline for a study of this kind.

Within this discipline, this particular study makes use of the four voices perspective in the theological action research (TAR) framework presented by Helen Cameron et al. in *Talking About God in Practice*.[3] The researcher shares Cameron et al.'s conviction and commitment to:

> the idea that the research done into faith practices [ought to be] "theological all the way through." This means that theology cannot appear after the data has been collected

---

2. Cameron et al., *Talking About God in Practice*, 52.
3. Cameron et al., *Talking About God in Practice*, 56–61.

as if it were simply "the icing on the cake already baked in the oven of social analysis." Rather, researchers employing [theological action research] consider all the material—written and unwritten, textual and practical—as (potentially) "theology," as "faith seeking understanding." This means that the practices participated in and observed are themselves bearers of theology.[4]

While this study is not action research, it follows in the footsteps of many other projects in practical theology that have "used the four voices outside of the TAR approach for data analysis or theological reflection."[5] In this study the four voices approach provides a way of both maintaining and categorizing the theological perspectives explored within the project from start to finish. The four voices, and their use within this project, are summarized as follows:

1. The Voice of Normative Theology (Scripture and Tradition)

An assumption is made that Scripture, as interpreted in alignment with the broad tradition of Christian faith, is authoritative, and thus normative.[6] Such perspective invites a dialectical process of healthy critique and accountability for faith practice and declaration. The reflective portions of this study appeal to the authority of the normative voice.

2. The Voice of Formal Theology (Academic)

---

4. Cameron et al., *Talking About God in Practice*, 54.

5. Dunlop, "Using the 'Four Voices,'" 294. A summary of how the four voices approach shaped both the methodology and findings of several non-TAR projects in practical theology is described in Dunlop, "Using the 'Four Voices,'" which includes Watkins, *Disclosing Church*; and Bosman, "Celebrating the Lord's Supper." Dunlop specifically notes the usefulness of the four voices in processing complex theological scenarios and developing theological praxis, despite the approach not being "originally envisaged as a theological reflection model" (305).

6. Complementing the perspective within this methodology, scriptural authority is likewise assumed by the PAOC (see the abbreviations page for the URL). SOET is the official doctrinal statement of the denomination; within the subsection "Bible," it affirms the PAOC's position on scriptural authority.

Throughout Christian tradition, the formal voice has sought to articulate, discuss, and challenge the definitions of normative theology through academically informed methods of critical inquiry. The formal voice can be seen in commentaries, written theological positions and doctrinal statements prepared by trained theologians. The researcher acknowledges that this study itself represents an example of the formal voice: an academic engagement of faith-in-practice, and an attempt to provide normative critique of the espoused and operant theology of a group. The literature reviewed for this study, as well as the PAOC's official theological documents (when authored by trained theologians) further represent the formal voice within this project.[7]

   3. The Voice of Espoused Theology (Sermons, Articles, Conference Talks, and Official Dialogue)

The commonly articulated (or "ecclesially normative") expression of faith represents the espoused theology of the group being studied.[8] Distinct from the formal voice, the espoused voice represents a group's interpretive perspective on normative and formal voices of theology. Sermons, public presentations (e.g., a keynote talk given by a credential holder at a PAOC conference), informal writing (e.g., articles in the *Pentecostal Testimony* or *Enrich* magazines), operations manuals and templates for church leadership, as well as conversational statements made in the course of one's duties (e.g., an admonishment from a district superintendent, or the assertion of a particular priority by a pastor in a church staff meeting), all represent the espoused voice of theology, either broadly or locally.

   4. The Voice of Operant Theology (Practices and Behaviours)

---

   7. The theological documents of the PAOC include SOET, which itself is a 2022 "refresh" of the earlier SOFET and reflects the denomination's current formal theological perspective. Recognizing this continuity is important for the analysis of historical clergy experiences, many of which occurred prior to 2022.

   8. Cameron et al., *Talking About God in Practice*, 58.

INTRODUCTION

Embedded within the official practices, common behavioural expressions, and actions tolerated within the community lies the operant theology of the group. In the absence of critical reflection, incongruencies between the operant voice of theology and the other voices may go unnoticed by the group. In this study, operant theology is identified through careful analysis of the common experiences expressed by research participants, and through the examination of official decisions and actions undertaken or tolerated by the PAOC as it relates to those experiences.[9]

Despite the clarity with which the TAR model defines the unique cadence of these four voices, they must not be taken to exist in singularity from one another. Rather, a key feature of the four voices approach is in the recognition of the interplay between the voices, and in particular, the symphonic quality that a disciplined application of the approach brings to theological reflection.

> We must be clear that these four voices are not discrete, separate from one another; each voice is never simple. We can never hear one voice without there being echoes of the other three.[10]

This is especially important given that the data collected may not always fit neatly into a singular category.

Take, for example, the official theological documents of the PAOC: not all position papers list their authors or contributors, and when contributors are listed, no academic credentials are provided.[11] Publicly available biographical information on named

9. Cameron et al., *Talking About God in Practice*, 57.
10. Cameron et al., *Talking About God in Practice*, 57.
11. The PAOC's position papers on authority (2010) and the equality of women and men in leadership (2018) do not list the names of their contributors (Study Commission, "Authority"; PAOC, "PAOC Statement Regarding Equality"). The position papers on contemporary apostles (2002), contemporary prophets and prophecy (2007), dignity of human life (2001), miracles and healings (2007), and secret orders (2006) contain a list of contributors but not their qualifications (Griffin et al., "Contemporary Apostles"; Hazzard et al., "Contemporary Prophets"; Social Concerns Committee, "Dignity of Human Life"; Richards et al., "Miracles and Healings"; Churchill et al., "Membership in Secret Orders"). Based on publicly available biographical information, it

5

contributors reveal varying levels of academic training, ranging from nondegree undergraduate ministry diplomas to doctoral degrees in theology.[12] As such, case-by-case discretion must be used when determining which official PAOC statements are indeed the voice of formal theology, and which would more accurately be categorized as the voice of espoused theology. While more recent publications, such as *Essential Truths: The PAOC Statement of Essential Truths Commentary*,[13] feature editors and contributors with recognized academic credentials clearly engaging in formal theological work, in other cases (such as position papers with mixed authorship and varying levels of "critical and historically and

---

appears that at the time of their publication, the "Contemporary Apostles," "Contemporary Prophets," and "Miracles and Healings" position papers all had at least one contributor with an academic doctorate.

12. The intention to include pastors and lay leaders as contributing voices in formulating official theological positions (and not only "trained theologians" per se) is a notable feature of the PAOC. This practice may be reflective of a desire to ground its perspectives within the more ordinary framework of the layperson, or it may be an extension the historical suspicion of "intellectual" voices within the movement, as demonstrated in the PAOC's 1979 *Report of the Committee on the Philosophy of Education*, which states:

"We question the wisdom of expansion into more advanced education to the hazard of diverting the emphasis of our revival movement from a basically spiritual, to an intellectual one. The PAOC standards and priorities must always take precedence over those of any other [academic] accrediting body" (as quoted in Hildebrandt, "Curriculum Development for Worship," 160).

This position illustrates the primacy of the ministry practitioner (one who is directly engaged in the evangelistic and revival work associated with the movement's roots) as central to the PAOC's self-identity; the echoes of which are broadly evident in the general superintendent's description of the true Pentecostal calling in a 2023 article, which suggests that it is the missional activity of Pentecostals that serves as the unifying center of the movement (Wells, "Aligned for Mission"). In this light, the public perception that one has engaged faithfully in the ministry work associated with the legacy of the Pentecostal movement ultimately endows practitioners who lack formal academic training with significant authority, at least equal to trained theologians, in multiple areas of leadership (in the eyes of lay leaders and other practitioners, perhaps even more authority) and may explain the intentionality of their inclusion on formal committees tasked with theological work.

13. Johnson et al., *Essential Truths*.

philosophically informed enquiry"),[14] identifying the voice can be challenging.[15] Thus some of the official theology of the PAOC may best be described as a mixture of formal and espoused voices claiming to be normative. Notwithstanding the significance of this dynamic in itself,[16] from a methodological standpoint Cameron et al. affirms that the overlapping of these categories and the presence of this type of complexity remains comfortably within the scope of the approach, where each voice is always "interrelated and overlapping."[17] Consequently, therein lies the strength of this method: the four voices are "a device for making this complexity manageable,"[18] by supplying a set of lenses for exploring the theology that permeates the entire inquiry without requiring that any of the dissonances and inconsistencies (which exist in all theological systems) become something else first.

---

14. Cameron et al., *Talking About God in Practice*, 58.

15. In addition to contributors with varying degrees of academic training, the position papers also vary in their academic quality. For example, Griffin et al., "Contemporary Prophets," prominently features engagement and commentary indicative of familiarity with the disciplines reflected in formal biblical studies; whereas Churchill et al., "Membership in Secret Orders," makes numerous broad and unqualified statements, assumes the interpretation of fourteen different Scripture references (without any context whatsoever), and appears unaware of any formal literature on the subject. As such, this collection of material is a mixed source: representation of the formal theological voice is interspersed with the espoused. Confusion may be further compounded by the genre of the documents themselves, which are intended to provide a normative critique for the operant theology of the denomination.

16. The participant narratives are indicative of a broad level of confusion in regard to what constitutes normative theology. Many participants described experiences of distress related to their deconstruction of espoused theological perspectives they had unquestioningly adopted at their induction into the PAOC. This phenomenon further underscores the need to promote practices of informed theological reflection within the PAOC as a whole.

17. Cameron et al., *Talking About God in Practice*, 56.

18. Cameron et al., *Talking About God in Practice*, 56.

Limitations

This study is designed to be indicative, not exhaustive. While the research question makes no assumption of abuse of power within the PAOC, when such experiences are recorded, they serve as indicators of the same. Notwithstanding, this study makes no claim to having engaged in an investigation of a judiciary nature, nor do the representations of participant data preclude the potential innocence of an individual named in the behaviours per se. Even when specific events are described in detail, only the participant's perspective has been captured. While the claims of participants have been verified as reasonably as possible based on their coherency, consistency with available known facts (such as dates, times, and locations), and the corroboration of other overlapping accounts within the sample, allegations of misconduct narrated by research participants were not presented to the persons named in those accounts for a response. As this is a formal academic inquiry, not a legal investigation, the overall conclusions reached are merely indicative of the need for further inquiry based on the presented findings.

Positionality of the Researcher

The perspective of the researcher is informed by critical realism, with the belief that one cannot be entirely free of bias but must instead identify and disclose positionality. As such, the researcher discloses that he is a Canadian Christian of mixed European and Indigenous ancestry; a heterosexual male of middle-class economic status, aged thirty-eight at the beginning of the project. He is an insider to the PAOC, holding clergy credentials onward from 2002, and having ministered in three PAOC Districts: Western Ontario (WOD), British Columbia and Yukon (BCYD), and Eastern Ontario (EOND). The author has familiarity with district and national personnel due to participation in multiple projects, including contract employment with the International Office (Mission Canada). The researcher's perspective is further impacted by

INTRODUCTION

his own experiences of power differentials in the PAOC, including but not limited to, coercion to sign an NDA and the felt impact of misconduct by multiple PAOC clergy in leadership roles over the course of twenty years (including lying, manipulation, threatening, breach of process, and passivity upon reporting mistreatment to the proper ecclesial authorities). The longevity and diversity of the researcher's pastoral work influences his perspective regarding the potentiality of systemic versus localized dysfunction in addition to inclining him toward sympathy for young pastors who are distraught over alleged mistreatment. As a staunch egalitarian (and having mentored a number of young women who have entered pastoral roles), the researcher is likewise influenced toward greater sensitivity to reported issues of sexism. The researcher's appearance most resembles that of a white or Caucasian person, with little visual cue of his Indigenous heritage, and therefore the researcher notes exceptionally limited experiences of personal racial discrimination, while also noting a broad awareness of the impact of racism on Indigenous people.

In consideration of this positionality, the researcher deliberately chose a semi-structured interview format with predetermined, open-ended questions in order to limit the influencing of interviewees based on the researcher's own bias (whether conscious or unconscious). Follow-up questions were based entirely on participant answers, and the researcher made no references to his own experiences during the interview process. Participants were asked to interpret their own answers to questions for greater clarity in order to further reduce interpretation bias.

Research Ethics

Prior to commencement, a research proposal was submitted to the Research Ethics Committee at London School of Theology, with approval to proceed being granted on March 8, 2022. To ensure the safety and well-being of participants, the interview questions and participant engagement process were screened by a registered psychotherapist with speciality in trauma and religious systems prior to commencement.

Analytic Approach

A general inductive approach, common in qualitative research, was employed for data analysis.[19] As there were no presupposed expectations of any particular findings, this method allowed conclusions to emerge "from the ground up, rather than handed down entirely from a theory or from the perspective of the inquirer."[20] The strength of this approach is in its ability to "condense extensive and varied raw text data into a brief, summary format," and to clearly articulate "transparent and defensible" connections between the research findings and the theories that emerge from open inquiry.[21] While other analytical approaches to the research question were initially evaluated (e.g., phenomenology, narrative analysis), a general inductive approach better fits both the specific objective of this research and the need for a flexible approach toward this first academic inquiry on the subject.

David R. Thomas, in an effort to summarize the particulars of this method (which he acknowledges may be slightly less familiar to researchers than other approaches), notes:

> The general inductive approach is most similar to grounded theory but does not explicitly separate the coding process into open coding and axial coding. As well, researchers using the general inductive approach typically limit their theory building to the presentation and description of the most important categories.[22]

While this study did, in fact, engage both open and axial stages of coding, the focus on broad trends most relevant to the research question (and thus the necessary condition of limiting data

---

19. Thomas, "General Inductive Approach," 238–39.
20. Creswell and Poth, *Qualitative Inquiry*, 22.
21. Thomas, "General Inductive Approach," 238.
22. Thomas, "General Inductive Approach," 241.

analysis to this narrow scope) is most accurately described as a general inductive analysis, as opposed to pure grounded theory.[23]

Notwithstanding, general inductive analysis is an especially appropriate approach for this study given the location of practical theology within the "interpretive-hermeneutical paradigm,"[24] which seeks not to impose a particular theological assumption onto a problem but rather to engage in some process of critical reflection.[25] Thus while the theories presented in this research emerge from the broad narrative represented by the complete list of codes (as opposed to a deductive-hypothesis approach),[26] the flexibility of a general inductive analysis allowed for a focused and thorough examination of only the most relevant themes, while yet maintaining a disciplined and methodical approach toward trustworthy conclusions.[27]

Selection Process and Demographics

Participants were primarily selected from respondents to a survey inviting participation. The survey was posted in the PAOC/NL Pastors Facebook group on June 13, 2022, an unofficial social media group comprised of 988 PAOC credential holders at the time

---

23. Corbin and Strauss, "Grounded Theory Research," 11, 17. While the research subjects were asked to interpret their own experiences (these descriptions were carefully used by the researcher for code cross comparison), and this data was used to generate the theories presented, the scope of this project included a practical limitation that precluded a formal theory verification process via second interviews. Thus while heavily influenced by grounded theory, the inability to engage "repeated interviews" for the inclusion of a detailed and critical analysis of the underlying theory (11) is another significant factor in rendering the description of this project most appropriately as a general inductive analysis.

24. Swinton and Mowat, *Practical Theology*, 75.

25. Swinton and Mowat, *Practical Theology*, 77–78. As noted, in this project the four voices model is used as a method for engaging in this process.

26. Biggs et al., *Research Methods*, 274.

27. Yvonna S. Lincoln and Egon G. Guba, *Naturalistic Inquiry*, as cited in Thomas, "General Inductive Approach," 243.

of writing.[28] This platform was chosen for its high saturation of PAOC clergy in addition to its arm's length distance from any official PAOC channels. Members of the group were given permission to share the survey link (which was public) with others outside the group, especially to those who were hard to reach (specifically, former clergy).

In order to develop a sample that is rich and varied, participants were selected not only on the basis of their interest in participation but also on the basis of their gender, age, race, region (PAOC district), and whether they were current or former credential holders. Due to minimal survey engagement from women, racial minorities, persons under the age of thirty, and former PAOC clergy, the researcher sought to add further diversity to the research sample by engaging in chain-referral sampling, a method useful for engaging "hard-to-reach" populations who might not identify their interest in participation due to "social stigma, concern for issues of confidentiality and fear of exposure because of possible threats to security," or if the research relates to a sensitive topic.[29] Whereas traditional snowball sampling may increase the risk of sampling bias, chain-referral sampling better manages this risk by imposing additional structure onto the referral process: the researcher independently engaged multiple sources with known contacts in the hard-to-reach population and contacted their referrals directly, without disclosing to the source whether their referral had been contacted or had agreed to participate.[30]

---

28. The group consisted of over 1000 members at the time the survey was posted and had 988 members as of January 26, 2024.

29. Penrod et al., "Discussion of Chain Referral," 100–101. While these concerns are cited in the context of medical research with stigmatized groups, the prominence of themes such as "fear of retaliation" and "marginalization" within the sample (see tables 2.1–2.3) demonstrates the need for the same level of care and sensitivity. Fear of reprisal (should their participation in this research be discovered) was most common for women, racial minorities, and young clergy. Despite the initial hesitation to be identified, these demographics were the most vocal in their support for the importance of this study, as well as in expressions of gratitude for the opportunity to participate.

30. Penrod et al., "Discussion of Chain Referral." In this study it was perceived that if those who had already participated in an interview were used to

INTRODUCTION

During interviews, participants sometimes provided the names of others whom they felt should also participate in the study (this was unprompted); however, no referrals from members of the sample group were interviewed at any stage of the research. A chart representing the recruitment method of the sample group, which includes the number of participants referred from each chain-referral source, is disclosed in fig. 1.1.

FIGURE 1.1 Participant Interviews by Recruitment Method[31]

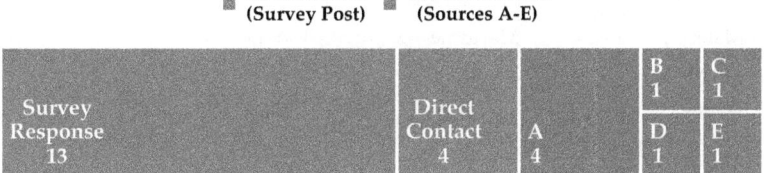

Interviews commenced on June 17, 2022, and proceeded in three stages as outlined in table 1.1. The sample pool increased in size through each stage of induction until the researcher was confident of saturation, which was first suspected after seventeen interviews, and was formally confirmed following the twenty-fifth interview.[32] The demographics of the sample group are provided in table 1.2.

---

identify other potential participants, they might influence those they recruited to interpret the open-ended questions in a particular way, or perhaps seek to recruit participants whose stories intersected with their own. By using chain-referral sampling instead of snowball sampling, the integrity of the participant pool was better managed.

31. Four participants were aware of the project and the interest survey posted to social media but made contact with the researcher directly (rather than completing the survey) and are noted as "direct contact." Of this group, three were part of the hard-to-reach population, and two indicated apprehension about completing the interest survey for privacy reasons. Participants from Chain Referral Source A were unknown to each other, without any overlapping employment or church affiliation, but hold in common the resignation of their clergy credentials and exit from ministerial service in the PAOC.

32. Saturation refers to the point at which the same themes and experiences

TABLE 1.1 Interview Stages

	Dates	Number of Interviews
Stage 1	June 2022—September 2022	12
Stage 2	December 2022—March 2023	7
Stage 3	April 2023—May 2023	6

TABLE 1.2 Research Participant Demographics

Five Views of the Sample Group				
Gender	Age	PAOC District	Race	Credentials
Male: 14 (56%) Female: 11 (44%)	20s: 5 30s: 11 40s: 6 50s: 2 60s: 1	Maritime—2 Quebec—1 Eastern Ontario—6 Western Ontario—5 Manitoba—1 Saskatchewan—2 Alberta & NWT—3 BC & Yukon—5	White—20 (80%) Non-white—5 (20%)	Current—18 (72%) Resigned—6 (24%)[33] Never held—1 (4%)[34]
Total: 25	Total: 25	Total: 25	Total: 25	Total: 25

are demonstrated consistently, with no new variations emerging. In this case, no new experience codes were generated after the seventeenth interview. In order to be assured saturation had been reached, the remaining two interviews in the second series were completed, and five more interviews were conducted in series three. These additional interviews demonstrated that saturation had indeed been achieved, while also providing a helpful thickness to the overall sample.

33. To preserve the integrity of this study, only those who resigned their credentials were eligible to participate. Respondents who had their credentials revoked due to a disciplinary process were excluded.

34. Due to a misunderstanding in the intake process, one participant was inducted for interview who had never held clergy credentials, despite having served for over fifteen years in significant ministerial roles with the PAOC. Following consultation with the researcher's supervisor, this interview was nonetheless included in the sample due to its material value, with this disclaimer provided as notice of the irregularity.

INTRODUCTION

INTERVIEW METHOD AND RESULTS

A semi-structured interview framework, reflective of the inductive approach of this project, was designed in order to facilitate the open exploration of interview questions related to the topic. The average interview lasted one hour and fifty-one minutes and produced an interview transcript of 17,977 words. In total, over forty-six hours of interview recordings were captured, yielding approximately 1178 pages of single-spaced twelve-point transcript. Notes, taken by the researcher during the interviews were also used in this project.

Confidentiality and Data Retention

In keeping with generally accepted practices of qualitative research, and the guidelines established by the Research Ethics Committee at London School of Theology, all participant data was destroyed after having satisfied the examiners of this study.

Pseudonyms are used to refer to all research participants in this study, and identifiable information has been redacted from their narratives. While the integrity and meaning of their experiences have been carefully preserved, in order to ensure confidentiality, any specific places, names, dates, or other details that could be associated with their identity have been modified or redacted prior to submission for examination.

Cooperation with the PAOC

The sensitivity of this research topic must be noted. Open-ended inquiries, such as this one, come with the risk that the answers recorded may not always present an institution in a favourable light. Therefore, as a matter of integrity and courtesy, the researcher engaged early on in a dialogue with the national leadership of the PAOC to share the focus of this study and discuss its potential implications.

The PAOC was a cooperative partner in this project, endorsing the value of the study, providing credential-change data, and inviting publication of the completed study in order to further assist the working group on abuse of power with their mandate.

CONTEXT AND BACKGROUND

The Pentecostal Assemblies of Canada

This study on power dynamics between members of the clergy initially emerged from a desire to study the impact of formal theology on operant (or "lived-out") theology; in particular, how a group's understanding of theological anthropology impacted the way they treated one another (interpersonal ethics) was of interest. The PAOC provides a remarkable context to examine this phenomenon. Unlike other denominations with lengthy doctrinal statements, the PAOC's recently updated "Statement of Essential Truths" (SOET) is a mere 1067 words, with the majority of text spent in sections on "The Triune God," "Salvation," and "Spirit Baptism."[35] Only twenty-two words are devoted to the expression of what it means to be a human being, and these are buried in a larger section on the doctrine of all creation:

> Formed in the image of God, both male and female, humankind is entrusted with the care of God's creation as faithful stewards.[36]

This sentence, true to the document title, conveys several "essential truths," namely that humans are made in God's image, as male and female, and possess an immutable vocational calling. While this statement succeeds in being both accurate and reflective of the broad theological tradition within which the PAOC finds itself, its brevity requires denominational adherents to provide their own interpretive framework and a contextual understanding of important concepts (e.g., image bearing). Further discussion on

35. Respectively, 181 words, 166 words, 116 words.
36. SOET, s.v. "Creation."

INTRODUCTION

humanity is limited to the text of Article 6, "Positions and Practices" of the PAOC General Constitution, which introduces one new anthropological statement from the previous version:

> We believe in the biblical teaching of God's original and ongoing design for humanity as two distinct sexes, male and female, determined by genetics.[37]

Notwithstanding the potential challenge of deference to genetics in a theological document,[38] this statement adds some dimensionality to the earlier position; whatever human beings are, at the very least the God who made them in his image was intentional about their form.

Theological Anthropology

It is noteworthy that while other doctrinal statements in the SOET feature further explanatory and interpretive material, these attempts at a theological anthropology do not. Of course, doctrinal statements are, by their nature, reductive: they aim to squeeze exhaustive material into a form that is clear and succinct for common use, while yet remaining truthful. Often, the determinate factor for the length or thoroughness of a particular section in a doctrinal statement has been the level of controversy (or lack thereof) around the subject. Historically, as the church has navigated conflict over particular tenets of faith, doctrinal statements have been revised and expanded as needed (for example, the Nicene Creed's expanded emphasis on Christ's divinity in the face

---

37. SOET, art. 6.4.

38. It was noted publicly by the researcher, in his comments from the floor during open discussion at the 2022 General Conference, that there are a variety of genetic anomalies that might make sexual differentiation difficult, including conditions where genetic testing returns with data at variance of typical XX or XY chromosomes. While rare, these conditions are well documented, and thus the author suggested that appealing to genetics as authoritative in this matter is not only insufficient but wholly inappropriate (giving consideration to the educational disciplines of the authors, who are theologians and not biologists).

of Arian controversy).[39] Reading the SOET through this historical lens, it would appear then that theological anthropology was neither a controversial nor particularly urgent subject to be reflected upon during the refreshing of the statement. An examination of the official SOET commentary, released in 2023, confirms that the pressing issue at the time of the revision was a "concern for creation care,"[40] and that with this perspective, the material was indeed intentionally reorganized to be less human-centric:

> This repeated focus on the whole creation, and the location of previously separate confessions about humanity, angels, and sin under Creation, puts more emphasis on God as Creator and on his work with all of creation, shifting SOET from an anthropocentric to a more broadly creational perspective.[41]

In general, it would be fair to critique the doctrinal anthropology of the PAOC as primarily a functional tool in the service of revival and evangelism activity; it is chiefly concerned with articulating humanity's sinfulness and the need for salvation.

While it could be noted that the PAOC's 2001 position paper, "Dignity of Human Life" makes uncharacteristically strong anthropological declarations, these statements are functionally tied to an argument against abortion and seem to represent the espoused theology of the PAOC regarding a specific social issue rather than the formal theology of the denomination more broadly.[42]

---

39. Shelley, "Splitting Important Hairs," 131.

40. Johnson et al., *Essential Truths*, 24.

41. Johnson et al., *Essential Truths*, 24. Notwithstanding the ecological priority reflected in the refreshed SOET, the updated statement is still an improvement over its predecessor, SOFET (2014), which contains a statement on humanity even less robust.

42. See Social Concerns Committee, "Dignify of Human Life," sec. 1, "The Human Person: Created in the Image of God."

INTRODUCTION

Abuse of Power

Simultaneous to the theological committee's work on the updated SOET, complaints of unaddressed abuses of power (allegedly perpetuated by PAOC clergy in positions of authority onto their subordinates) had also prompted the formation of a special working group. Tasked with providing recommendations to the general executive, the Working Group on Abuse of Power contributed to the development of resolution 20, presented at a special general meeting on April 21, 2022, and proposing that "abuse of power or authority" should be added to by-law 10.6.2.1.1.3 as an example of a moral or ethical failure that disqualifies a pastor from ministry.[43] The vote to adopt the resolution passed; a milestone that occurred just weeks prior to the adoption of the updated SOET at the Fifty-Fifth General Conference in Winnipeg.

The proximity of these two moments underscores the significance of the intersection between theological anthropology and interpersonal ethics. To use the language of the four voices, it underscores the importance of a dialectic theological model where operant theology emerges from a reflective process. The relationship between a doctrinal statement that pays minimal attention to theological anthropology, and a corresponding organizational culture with a reactionary amendment regarding abuse of power, forms the context of this study.

The Cost of Dissonance

As the data will show, an integrated application of the PAOC's doctrinal statements on anthropology, as minimal as they are, are conspicuously missing from the events described by the research participants in regard to their experiences. The frequency and magnitude of the grievances expressed within the sample group over mistreatment further imply that, at the very least, there is a dissonance between normative and operant theological anthropology within the denomination.

43. PAOC, "Special Meeting Minutes," 22–25.

Whether these problems proceed from a lack of formal emphasis on intrinsic human value, a distorted understanding of hierarchy and submission, or merely the absence of metrics for calculating the human impact of key decisions, the costs of the behaviours that have been documented in this study are immense. While individual clergy who have experienced serious harm at the hands of leadership must navigate the impact of such a profound betrayal, the entirety of the constituency likewise bears a cost. The relationship between clergy well-being and an overall decline in the number of clergy in service raises significant questions about future sustainability, should these problems go unaddressed. It is therefore the goal of this study to present an informed theological reflection on the data collected as the basis of a model for renewed praxis.

2

Findings

CHAPTER OVERVIEW

THE VOLUME OF THIS data and the sensitivity of the subject factor into the task of presenting an account of its collective meaning. Generalizing and abridging complex experiences that were (in many cases) shared for the very first time, often punctuated with tears, without somehow violating a sacred trust is a difficult task. In order to honour these narratives while simultaneously engaging in critical analysis of their content and their overlapping themes, the researcher has endeavoured to include as many summaries and direct quotes as can be manageably contained within this chapter. In reference to the four voices, the descriptions of experiences marked by power differentials recounted in this study are a way of accessing the operant voice of theology in the PAOC. Collectively, these narratives provide a way to observe how empowered clergy have actually acted,[1] and in doing so they reveal something about

---

1. Throughout this study, the term *empowered clergy* is used to describe ministers who were in a position of power over another. The term *subordinate clergy* is used as a corresponding indicator of a minister who was not in a position of power.

the way espoused and formal theological views are, or are not, integrated into practice.[2]

The descriptions of events and experiences documented here stem from a simple, open-ended question: "Have you had any significant experiences you could share with me?" The experiences recounted were carefully coded with an appropriate descriptor to allow for a cross comparison of like events throughout the sample. The coded experiences are further organized according to categories taken from Christopher Steed's 2017 book, *Smart Leadership—Wise Leadership*: indifference, inequality, and indignity.[3]

The complete list of codes are provided in tables 2.1, 2.2, and 2.3, and include short definitions.[4] The frequency of common experiences, tracked across the entire sample, allows these codes to be ranked and listed in an order that reflects their prominence. Factors such as the magnitude of an experience and the personal impact of the event are considered in the ranking process.[5] It is important to note that this ranking does not represent a strictly mathematical analysis, as making such a calculation from qualitative data would be impractical. Challenges such as overlapping occurrences of the same code within an interview, and the roles played by multiple persons would make a purely quantitative ranking of experiences

2. As Cameron et al. emphasize, even when actions appear to lack embedded theology, this is itself an operant theology that must be examined (*Talking About God in Practice*, 54–55, 60–61).

3. Steed, *Smart Leadership*, 88. In keeping with the methodological parameters of this research, an inductive approach was maintained throughout the process of interviewing and coding. Steed's categories were identified as a compatible and effective means of organizing the findings subsequent to the coding and analysis being completed.

4. This naming and defining of experiences is central to the work of this project. As Cameron et al. note, embedded in practical theology is the "discovering and forming [of] language for the often hidden depths of what [is observed]. This language—or naming—enables better the necessary conversation between embodied and formal or normative theologies; and it makes possible a wider sharing of the meanings made real in practical Christian faith" (*Talking About God in Practice*, 61).

5. For example, experiencing a singular berating comment versus repetitive instances of the same for months, or the severity of an experience as interpreted by the participant.

Findings

misleading. The rankings provided in the tables should therefore be used as indicators of the types of experiences clergy endure, and their occurrence within the sample (while also recognizing that a single, complex event can have multiple codes). A quantitative analysis of the suspected frequencies of these types of experiences across the entire PAOC clergy base remains a project for future researchers, and is not speculated here. While all data, down to the smallest detail, is significant,[6] what follows is a carefully arranged presentation and analysis of the data with special attention given to the codes that bear particular significance within the theme and scope of the research question.

As a preface to this material, a short analysis of declining clergy numbers in the PAOC is provided. Finally, despite being far less prominent than other codes, a special note on illegal behaviour with a corresponding table of codes (table 2.4) is included prior to the chapter conclusion, as the seriousness of this material necessitates specific mention.

AN AUTOPSY OF DECLINING CLERGY RETENTION

PAOC Clergy Changes, 2017–22

The term "clergy crisis" is ubiquitous with declining Bible college and seminary enrolments, and the dwindling enthusiasm of young pastors within once vibrant evangelical movements; both challenges are well-documented realities facing the PAOC.[7] As published in the PAOC's "2022 Fellowship Statistics" report, during the five-year period from 2017 to 2022 the total number of active clergy in the PAOC decreased by 259, or roughly 7.5 percent overall.[8] Compared against Canada's total population growth of 7.5 percent

---

6. Both from a methodological standpoint as well as from the personal standpoint of the research participants.

7. Wilkinson and Ambrose, *After the Revival*, 252.

8. PAOC, "2022 Fellowship Statistics," 1.

over the same period,[9] it is reasonable to surmise that the largest Pentecostal movement in Canada is indeed facing a concerning shortage of clergy that shows no sign of immediate improvement. When discussing the causes of this problem, low enrolment in denominational schools is commonly expressed as the primary factor,[10] with generational shifts in values earning an honourable mention.[11] A basic analysis of the data in the PAOC Credential Change Reports casts significant doubt on these assumptions.

As fig. 2.1 illustrates, when comparing new credentials issued versus the number of clergy lost to either death or dismissal during this five-year period, the PAOC achieved a net gain of 335 clergy.[12] On its own, this would represent a 9 percent gain, which would have exceeded population growth over the same time period if it were the only factor.

In contrast, over the same period the number of existing credential holders who moved to inactive status, resigned credentials, or lapsed (nonrenewal), massively outweighed the number of clergy who reactivated or reinstated their credentials, after having done the same.[13] It is this phenomenon that bears special relevance for this study: if the retention rate of credential holders reflected the same ratio as "new credentials vs death & dismissal," the PAOC would have seen a net increase of 200 credential holders from 2017 to 2022, (a growth rate of 5.3 percent) instead of the staggering net loss of 259 (decline of 7.5 percent).[14]

---

9. According to Statistics Canada for reference periods 2017 to 2024 (https://www150.statcan.gc.ca/t1/tbl1/en/tv.action?pid=1710000901).

10. Wilkinson and Ambrose, *After the Revival*, 252; and private source.

11. Often rooted in an uncritical extrapolation of Millennial and Gen-Z church attendance data, assertions are made that younger Christians are less likely to value pastoral work, at least in its present form. See Erlacher and White, *Mobilizing Gen Z*, 86–87.

12. *Dismissal* refers to clergy whose credentials are revoked for disciplinary reasons.

13. The term *lapsed* here includes those who did not renew their clergy credentials by choice (as an alternative to formal resignation) or negligence (e.g., missing a fee deadline).

14. The transfers of clergy in and out of the PAOC to associated

FINDINGS

FIGURE 2.1 PAOC Clergy Credential Changes, 2017–22[15]

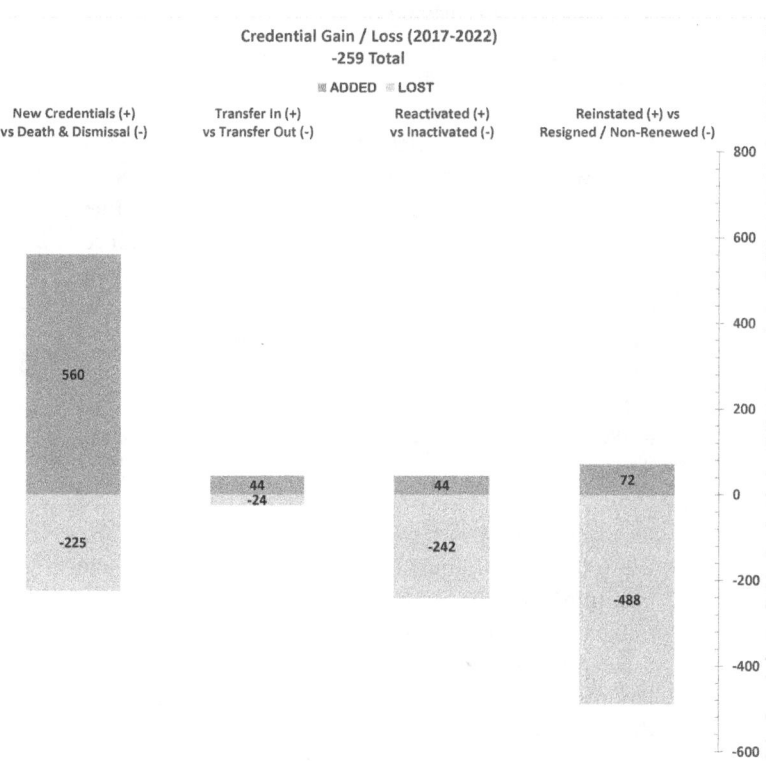

Qualitative Indications

While additional analysis and modelling may provide further insight, the qualitative data collected in this study provides an account of prevalent experiences which are indicative of this rate of withdrawal, resignation, and nonrenewal. Examining accounts of the circumstances of resignation (or its consideration) thus may serve as a type of autopsy for the observed decline.[16]

---

denominational bodies in another countries bear less relevance within this analysis.

    15. Source data provided by PAOC Clergy Records Department on June 23, 2022.

    16. Participants indicated that nonrenewal was an effective form of soft

[They all knew I was being mistreated, but] nobody even cared to pick up the phone and say, "Hey, how are you?" So I ended up just leaving . . . I let my credentials pass. I said, "Forget it, I'm out . . . I'm done with it."
And I got a phone call after there was a survey about credential holders under thirty, and the lack thereof. [Someone at the district] called me up and he says, "Hey, we noticed that your credentials have expired." I said, "You're just calling me now? Over a year after they lapsed? . . . I don't even live [in your district] anymore. You have no idea where I am in the world, because [none of you] care."
. . . I never heard from anybody [in the district] ever again. That was it. That was the end of my relationship with the PAOC.
—*Wayne (former PAOC credential holder, eight years of Service)*[17]

It's really messed with my head . . . I love ministry, and I love the church, [but] I have a really, really hard time imagining myself continuing. I've been in situations, time and time again, where I'm not heard, and I'm not listened to, and [other PAOC clergy] use me. And now I'm just at a point where I ask, "What for?" . . . I know that I could go elsewhere and be appreciated, and be compensated fairly, [and] be part of a better work culture. So why put myself in this situation over and over and over again?
—*Diane (current PAOC credential holder, ten years of service)*[18]

Looking back, [I said to myself], "Yes, I have credentials . . . but what is it really doing for me?" [The PAOC] should have been like a union. They should have been the people that said, "Hey, how is this? How is this

---

resignation, perhaps because the active participation in the resignation process required further perceived contact with clergy in positions of power.

17. Interview transcript.
18. Interview transcript.

functioning? How are we going to help young pastors who get taken advantage right away?"
... It's not what I would have ever expected. And I think that's part of why I haven't gone back to ministry. In all honesty, it was both my internship church and my first job [in a PAOC church]. They were very similar, working for somebody who [belittled and took advantage of me.]
—*Cynthia (former PAOC credential holder, three years of service)*[19]

I grew up in a generation where if you just did what your superiors said, that would be the right thing to do. So, I did [that] . . . but I [was blacklisted anyway]. For years, I carried with me the guilt that it was my fault. And there was no one, no one to walk me through what I was feeling.
. . . I carried the scars of [being abused by that church] and [subsequently being marginalized by the district superintendent] and I had no one who called me. No one to say, "Ross, how are you doing?" And wow. I know there were a lot of [pastors] in similar situations; people who would have left ministry and even their relationship with God altogether.
—*Ross (current PAOC credential holder, forty years of service)*[20]

Each of these narratives emerges from a failure to create what Christopher Steed refers to as "environments of value."[21] In a study on the impact of workplace dynamics on individuals, he observed that "participants in an organisation flourish when, under the right conditions, the inner value they live out in the workplace is converted to external, added value."[22] Empirically speaking, these valuing environments create not only high levels of productivity but also high levels of satisfaction among their participants, leading to retention.[23] Institutions that foster internal cultures

19. Interview transcript.
20. Interview transcript.
21. Steed, *Smart Leadership*, 82.
22. Steed, *Smart Leadership*, 83.
23. Steed, *Smart Leadership*, 83.

of human dignity, mutual respect, and fair compensation flourish; those that fail to do so, do not.[24] It is reasonable, therefore, to investigate whether organizations experiencing a declining retention of their workforce (such as the PAOC) are experiencing the predictable consequences of a non-valuing environment and not merely the tertiary effects of market trends beyond their control. Steed continues:

> The question I set out to answer stemmed from intrigue. Why were client narratives, often of distress arising from experiences within organizations, generating statements about human value or its erosion? . . . I began to listen out for client reports to do with 12 perceptions of feeling: belittled or put down, diminished, bullied, "trashed," useless, disrespected, not noticed or disregarded, not heard, passed over, rejected, discriminated against, insulted.[25]

Steed's observations about his client's language in relation to their workplaces bear a remarkable resemblance to many of the descriptions provided by participants of this study as they described their experiences with other members of the clergy. Take for example the broader dynamics of Wayne's story; in particular, the multiple accounts of mistreatment that ultimately led to his resignation and credential nonrenewal.

---

24. Steed, *Smart Leadership*, 46. Steed's analysis of the impact such failures have on public image (and resultant deficits of trust and goodwill within their communities) is especially relevant within the broader sociological context of religion in the present era. As Matthew Guest points out, the impact of marketization of evangelical Christianity brings with it an expectation that church and denominational leaders will "take advantages of the processes of commodification common in commercial settings" such as branding, packaging, production, and marketing (Guest, *Neoliberal Religion*, 68, 61–70). Ironically, this methodology may have a cooling effect on the perceived urgency of the normative anthropological priorities embedded in the Christian faith; to whatever extent that "processes of commodification" might lead to the profitable and efficient mistreatment of employees, marketized religious institutions may thus expose themselves to even greater levels of scrutiny from their newfound markets, which, as Steed alludes, expect public accountability from corporate entities, especially the equitable treatment of human beings.

25. Steed, *Smart Leadership*, 87.

FINDINGS

My contract had me working over fifty hours a week as a youth pastor, but I soon realized I was making a lower wage per hour than the college students we hired to do small jobs around the church. That was the first time I felt exploited. And I couldn't just talk about wages openly, because if you do that you're seen as being ungrateful; like, the culture in the PAOC is that if you ever say you're wanting more money, you're crossing a line theologically. But exploited is the right word. I was working so much and I couldn't afford anything. And then the district superintendent called to ask me to volunteer with some church-plants. He said, "We can't afford to pay you, but you're talented and we need your help." That's what it was like. Once I was actually told that I wasn't even the first choice for my job, but I was hired because I was "cheap."

Race is another thing. My district was very happy to use me if they needed a token [racial minority] pastor, but they didn't actually see me as valuable enough to invest in financially or relationally. That's the culture of the PAOC. For example, I ended up working at [a different church], and my first week on the job I found out I was hired solely for racial diversity on the otherwise white staff. In my first staff meeting, in front of everyone, the lead pastor blindsided me by asking, "So now we have a lot of [my race] in the community, but they don't come to our church. What do we do?" At yet another church where I worked, my lead pastor compared my appearance to that of a "terrorist" [due to my race]. And that's bad, but these problems go further than race.

It's also the unchecked abuse of power. I've had more than one lead pastor express that I (as a single adult) needed their permission about who I date. I had another demand I get his approval on where I was allowed to rent. I've been yelled at so badly that I was later given a raise in pay on the condition I don't ever tell anybody what he said. Another time a lead pastor heard I had been offered a job elsewhere, so he fired me on the spot. I think because he felt that even hearing about another job was disloyal. I then had no choice but to take that job, even though it was at a church I wasn't totally sure I wanted to work at.

This has all broken me. It's messed me up. And that's why I left the PAOC. All this talk about "we're a family." No, we're not. The district knew how each of these pastors were behaving, [those pastors] had a track record of doing this to others, but [the district] never warned me about it and they never got involved. So I left.[26]

A Systemic Problem

Wayne's story is unfortunately not unique in the sample; in fact, most participants reported enduring overlapping experiences of mistreatment. While the settings of participant narratives span all eight PAOC districts (and in most cases, participants would not even know one another),[27] many cite the same person or persons as perpetrators of abuses of power in alarmingly similar ways. The collective narratives of the sample group produced a list of fifty-three different credential holders in positions of power or authority who engaged in unethical, and personally damaging, treatment of subordinates. Ten of the twenty-five participants independently and specifically named an unofficial "PAOC Old Boys Club" in allegations of abuse of power, with others alluding to the same.[28] Regarding individuals, fig. 2.2 illustrates the number of different research participants who named the same person in a complaint during their interview.

26. Summary of Wayne's story; edited for length and for confidentiality.
27. Due to geographic distance, demographic variance, and nonoverlapping chronology, most participants would likely be entirely unaware of each other's experiences.
28. The "PAOC Old Boys Club" is characterized as a loose and informal camaraderie of "insider" white male credential holders who share an absolute loyalty to "old-school" PAOC values. This group is suggested to have an inappropriate amount of hidden influence on the hiring and promotion of other clergy, in addition to being able to secure preferential treatment at will (including the dismissal of complaints) by sidestepping formal processes and appealing to insider connections.

Findings

FIGURE 2.2 Different Complaints Named per Person[29]

Persons named by:
■ 6 Individuals ■ 4 Individuals ■ 3 Individuals ■ 2 Individuals ■ 1 Individual

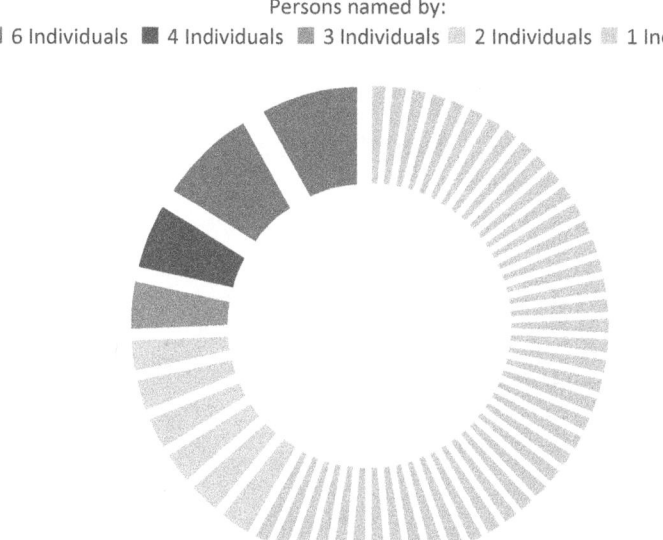

Considering the distance of time and space over which these narratives take place, and the broad consistency of their content, the overlapping data indicates that abuse of power has been persistent for some time, with named perpetrators comfortable in both their roles and behaviour. Regardless of official statements, sentiments expressed at conferences, or encouraging words within monthly newsletters, the participant accounts of unaddressed mistreatment by other members of the clergy are a sobering measure of a significant problem.

Dominant Themes for Categorizing Experiences

As mentioned, each of the coded experiences within this study fits squarely within one of the three categories: indifference, inequality,

---

29. A further eleven individuals were named as passive enablers in the face of clear abuses of power.

POWER IN PRACTICE

and indignity.[30] These three categories can be best understood not as three independent classifications but rather as three related (and sometimes overlapping) experiences.

FIGURE 2.3 Overlap of Themes

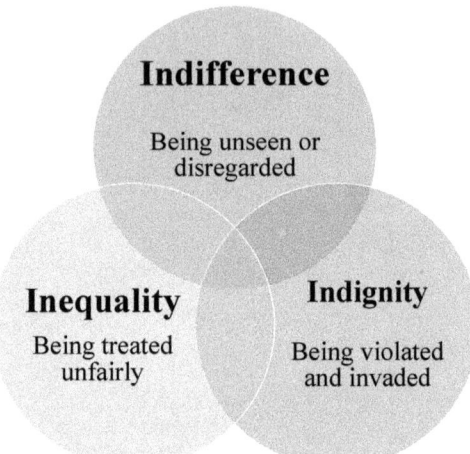

While each of the coded experiences has been associated to one primary category (e.g., favouritism is most obviously an issue of inequality), participants ascribed the most severe and negative impacts of their experiences to events that fell within a combination of multiple categories (e.g., suffering under inequality but having their complaint met with indifference, followed by an experience of indignity via direct retaliation, from the original party, after filing a complaint).[31] What follows is an exploration of each category and the coded experiences associated to it.

---

30. Steed, *Smart Leadership*, 87.

31. Notwithstanding the multiplied impact of overlapping categories, it must be noted that each of these experiences is dehumanizing in some form, and likely constitutes an abuse of power.

FINDINGS

INDIFFERENCE

For indifference to thrive, a workplace (or, in this case, the ecclesial structure of the PAOC) merely requires a system where those in a position of power are not held accountable for a failure to see those they lead as valuable humans.[32] Through the act of seeing and hearing those around them,[33] healthy leaders demonstrate that those they lead are valuable; in contrast, when leaders fail to do this, the effect on an individual is that they come to believe they are "undervalued, or of little worth," within the organization.[34] Thus even when indifference is practised unintentionally, its impact remains significant.[35]

In contrast, intentional forms of indifference are exhibited in callous or premeditated acts such as decisions to intentionally marginalize someone, or to patronize someone by giving the illusion of listening to them while harbouring prejudicial determinations. The calculated silencing of a person, through exclusion or

---

32. Steed, *Smart Leadership*, 88.

33. Steed, *Smart Leadership*, 86–88. Steed argues that listening must be done well for it to be effective. A leader's "listening" is not effective if the member they are listening to does not feel heard. Note that this does not require leaders to begin the uncontested implementation of all suggestions from those in subordinate roles; listening to a subordinate is not synonymous with agreeing or deferring to them. Nonetheless, authentic listening does require effectively seeing those one supervises as valuable and worth hearing. Practically, this may require an adjustment to one's weekly schedule or the development of new systems in order to effectively create room for this responsibility.

34. Steed, *Smart Leadership*, 88. For example, when an inexperienced director renders certain pastors in their area invisible (perhaps they aren't self-aware enough to realize that they "notice" only workers who are outgoing and tall) or when the DE fails to hold accountable a superintendent who repeatedly looks past the needs of those around them (some leaders are so focused on mission that they fail to see the human impact of their decisions). These deficiencies, though passive, have a significant impact on subordinate clergy.

35. A sense that indifference is often unintentional was captured in the ambivalent sentiments of participants who described the pain of an unjust experience while also releasing key authority figures from blame. Several participants described knowing that certain denominational leaders "meant well," despite simultaneously airing frustration over their refusal to act or intervene in a dire situation.

interruption, is especially devastating, as "to be human is to have a voice."[36] In all cases, indifference is dehumanizing and therefore has negative consequences for the organizations in which it occurs, both visibly (indifference negatively effects employee productivity and retention)[37] and invisibly (indifference erodes the spiritual integrity of the organization).

It is the latter that Christian institutions must become especially concerned with. Those that proclaim human beings as divine image bearers,[38] "cracked eikons, but eikons nonetheless,"[39] and those who are "bought at a price" (1 Cor 6:20) must recognize that these statements demand the practice of an integral Christian ethic that demonstrates human value regardless of a person's power or status.

Ranking Common Experiences of Indifference

The following table provides a ranked list of coded experiences of indifference. The list is divided into two columns: local church experiences[40] and systemic experiences.[41] In both cases, the referenced events have taken place specifically in the context of a power differential, with the empowered member of the clergy identified as directly responsible for the coded experience.[42]

---

36. Langberg, *Redeeming Power*, 7.
37. Steed, *Smart Leadership*, 88.
38. SOET, s.v. "Creation."
39. McKnight, *Community Called Atonement*, 75.
40. Local church experiences list codes associated with a local church ministry, in which a subordinate clergy member has suffered the indicated experience with a supervising member of the clergy (e.g., a youth pastor and a lead pastor).
41. Systemic experiences are occurrences that took place outside of the local church, which can include pastors in any role interacting with a district or national leader, a member of their DE or DLT, or another person of influence from outside of a congregational context.
42. The term *leader* is regularly used as shorthand to denote the empowered member of the clergy.

FINDINGS

TABLE 2.1 Common Experiences of Indifference

EXPERIENCES OF INDIFFERENCE (CODES AND PREVALENCE)			
Local Church Experiences		**PAOC/Systemic Experiences**	
Experiences of indifference that occurred specifically within a local church context (e.g., church staff interactions)		Experiences of indifference that occurred beyond the local church context (e.g., district and national interactions)	
CODE	**RANK**	**CODE**	**RANK**
Conflict of Interest	1	**Passivity**	1
The experience of being dismissed or disregarded due to a leader's conflict of interest (e.g., personal friendship) and associated prejudice		The experience of reporting a serious issue to a person in authority who determines not to act or intervene despite their capacity to do so	
Gaslighting	2	**Conflict of Interest**	2
The experience of being dismissed or disregarded due to a leader's repetitive denial and insistent reframing of the other person's experience		The experience of being dismissed or disregarded due to a leader's conflict of interest (e.g., personal friendship) and associated prejudice	
Conflict Avoidance	3	**Marginalization**	3
The experience of being dismissed or disregarded due to a leader's preference to avoid conflict		The experience of being intentionally isolated, preemptively dismissed or disregarded for opportunities as an informal sanction	
Tokenism	4	**Cover-Up Scheme**	4
The experience of being disregarded, despite one's status or position, due to the disingenuousness of the appointment (e.g., being placed on a lead team as a token woman, and never being taken seriously)		The experience of having the truth of an incident intentionally obfuscated by a person in authority (this may also result in the diminishing of one's personal credibility)	
		Lack of Clergy Support	5
		Experiencing the unavailability of support resources in the aftermath of a serious issue (e.g., inability to access counselling benefits)	

		Unaddressed Patterns	6
		The experience of harm from a leader who is known by district or national leaders to have engaged in such acts before (but has not been addressed)	
		Authoritarianism	7
		The experience of being, or having one's needs, preeminently dismissed and disregarded by a leader who is grossly misusing their position	
		Protectionism	8
		The experience of being dismissed or disregarded due to the priority of image management or self-protection (e.g., the risk of legal liability upon acknowledgment)	
		Tokenism	9
		The experience of being disregarded, despite one's status or position, due to the disingenuousness of the appointment (e.g., being placed on a lead team as a token woman, and never being taken seriously)	
		NDAs	10
		The experience of being silenced from communicating about a significant matter through a legally binding agreement (sometimes in exchange for severance)[43]	

43. In this context, NDAs are tracked only if they were used to limit a person's ability to share an experience of power abuse. While the use of NDAs in Canada has long been contested in certain circumstances, the 2023 decision by the Canadian Bar Association to prohibit the use of NDAs as a tool to hide abuse, harassment, and discrimination will have significant future impact on this practice. See Bhat and Schmunk, "Lawyers Across Canada."

	Withholding Information	11
	The experience of being disregarded and disadvantaged through the deliberate withholding or concealment of relevant information to which one is entitled (e.g., a lack of transparency regarding information attained in an exclusive meeting, to which the effected party cannot thus respond)	
	Abandonment	12
	The experience of being relationally cut off by members of the organization, despite retaining clergy credentials	
	Gaslighting	13
	The experience of being dismissed or disregarded due to a leader's repetitive denial and insistent reframing of the other person's experience	

Due to the volume of codes, the subsequent discussion will focus on the most prevalent experiences and their implications.

Systemic Passivity in the PAOC

Of particular note in this sample is the domination of the code "passivity." Twenty-two of the participants made a collective seventy-two references to experiences of passivity (often in multiple contexts) that impacted them in a significantly negative way. For example, when John became acutely aware of ethical breaches perpetuated by multiple district officers, including his district superintendent, he approached a member of the DE,[44] which functions

---

44. Notwithstanding that some districts have an equivalent body referred to as the DLT, DE is used in this study to refer to the body of elected credential holders that form the official governing board within a district, as specified in their constitution and by-laws.

as the official board of directors for the regional PAOC district, according to its by-laws.

> I reached out to [executive team member], and they didn't want to hear anything about it. They were like, "Nope, that's not my responsibility. I don't want to hear about it. Our purview is vision and budget." That raised red flags to me, like, yes, I get vision and budget, but where is the accountability? Some of the things that I had assumed for a long time were in place were not. We entrust the DE we have elected to provide accountability in these situations, but they don't.[45]

Dave, a youth pastor, had been enduring increasingly demeaning comments for months from his lead pastor, even being threatened with termination due to dislike of his preaching style. When he was suddenly (and inconsiderately) saddled with additional duties, his pastor admitted this was a calculated decision made for the purpose of "testing" him. Appalled, he addressed his supervisor directly, a confrontation that led to a season of aggressive gaslighting. Manipulated by insecurities that developed from his pastor's frequent reports about what congregants and board members were saying behind his back, he grew more and more depressed. Upon discovering that these disparaging comments were entirely fabricated, Dave confided the totality of the situation to the district superintendent, providing details and evidence of the misconduct (including the names of board members who had been pulled into the conflict). After taking in the account, the district superintendent's instructions were that he needed to "be a David to your Saul."[46] Despite being educated in a PAOC college,

---

45. Condensed from interview transcript.

46. This specific phrase is commonly used as a shorthand reference to Gene Edwards's book, *Tale of Three Kings*. Edwards's work is deeply embedded in the cultural framework of the PAOC in regard to power, submission, and abuse, and is frequently alluded to within the sample. This quote is an allusion to the theme of the book, which argues that a truly godly leader must never strike back at one in a position of spiritual authority, no matter how abusive their behaviour may be. In this case, the superintendent is suggesting that the path forward for this young pastor is to serve his leader faithfully, dodging but

Findings

attending ordination training through his district, and engaging his superintendent, Dave was never informed that he could have filed a complaint against the lead pastor for his actions, which were a clear violation of ministerial ethics.[47] Reflecting broadly on this experience, he noted:

> In all of these situations, there have been no repercussions for lead pastors or district leaders. I even reached out afterward to the general superintendent and shared my story with him. I said, "Something needs to change. And I'd love to be a part of that conversation." His response was very carefully passive. I realized that I wasn't going to get anywhere because I don't have a position of authority that needs to be paid attention to.[48]

While one can hardly fault a district or general officer for proceeding cautiously in the face of a complaint for which they have little context, it is clear that passivity (as a practice of indifference) is not limited to shrouded complaints with circumstantial evidence.

As a young youth pastor, Gary was let go by his church suddenly and without cause, following the resignation of the lead pastor.[49] Gary was instructed to continue in his job for a period of time, informed that this arrangement was his notice in lieu of severance, but was forbidden from telling anyone that he had been let go (despite receiving written notice). Several clear breaches of law followed. Prior to his conclusion, the church garnished his wages for costs associated with Gary's move to the church (years before), claiming these funds were "repayable loans" (a designation made without his knowledge nor his presence in a board meeting after his start date). At a time of the board's choosing,

---

not resisting any perceived attacks. This particular book, its message, and its influence are explored directly in ch. 4.

47. PAOC, "Ministerial Code of Ethics."

48. Paraphrased from interview transcript.

49. According to the statutes in the province of his employment, termination without cause is allowed as long as notice or severance is provided.

Gary was required to read a letter of resignation, despite the fact that he had not resigned. Following his termination, the Record of Employment (ROE) filed with the federal government was falsified to support the narrative, listing "Code E: Quit" as the reason for Gary's unemployment, instead of "Code M: Dismissal," making him ineligible for employment insurance benefits. When he approached the assistant superintendent (who was overseeing the church transition) about these legal and ethical breaches, he was discouraged from taking action.[50]

> [He told me], "You're a hotheaded young guy, you're getting burnt really bad. You could turn around and burn the church down [but] if you do that, you'll never work in a PAOC church again." The idea was [I'm supposed to] just grin and bear it, and God will reward [me] later . . . Looking back? It's [all about] protecting the church at all costs. And I get that side of it, except when the leadership of the church is toxic, and there's no accountability there! Like if you truly want to protect the church, then remove the toxic leadership, right? . . . [They say] "Churches are autonomous, and they can do what they want. We're a fellowship, we're not a denomination." Isn't that just skirting responsibility? . . . So we have to let them be autonomous? They're abusive! It's not autonomy, it's abuse![51]

Gary makes a formidable argument that underlines the issue of passivity within the sample frame. Yet this passivity is selective. While the sentiment that the district "cannot intervene" is often evoked in conversations with non-lead pastors, those serving in

---

50. It is important to note the obvious conflict of interest in this situation; the district, via the assistant superintendent, is charged with supporting and guiding a PAOC-affiliated church through a process of lead pastor transition. However in this case, the assistant superintendent's responsibility to the church conflicts with his responsibility to the credential holder, who is alleging mistreatment. The use of positional influence to discourage the credential holder from taking legal action (which, arguably, would reflect terribly on the district leader overseeing the transition), should be classified as an abuse of power due to this conflict of interest.

51. Interview transcript.

FINDINGS

lead roles experience a different reality. Albert, a lead pastor with seventeen years' experience, explains it this way:

> The district claims that local churches are autonomous but also manipulates them by dictating a "standard process" and the board really doesn't know any better. Yes, the church is technically autonomous, and it has the right to lead according to what they think is best in this situation, but the power dynamic between the district superintendent and the church board mean they are very easily manipulated.[52]

Another lead pastor, recounting a conflict with the district superintendent after their local church board made a decision, noted:

> When I pushed back on the district superintendent's objections and said, "This isn't the district's role, we are a fellowship of autonomous churches," he tried to intimidate me. I think he said something like, "Well, it is in *your* best interest to follow the advice of your superintendent."[53]

These stories, and those like them, are associated with multiple codes in table 2.1 that highlight the dark side of institutional indifference, not least of which include the obvious concerns demonstrated in these examples: conflict of interest, cover-up schemes,[54] and protectionism.[55] While failures to effectively respond to requests for help may constitute a passive form of indifference, they are nonetheless damaging.

52. Interview transcript.

53. Condensed from interview transcript S1P9. Emphasis added to reflect tone.

54. Ultimately, Gary's congregation was never told the truth about his departure; the accounts related by both lead pastors in this section involve significant attempts to "control the narrative" of events, both through pressures to sign an NDA for settlement and in significant withholding of information.

55. There is a pattern of prioritizing the preservation of the church's image; it often necessitates ignoring a cry for help from a member of the clergy. As will be explored in ch. 4, this is an example of sacralizing the image of an institution, perhaps falsely equating it with God's own reputation and in the process profaning that which is made in his own image (human beings).

Marginalization and Victim Blaming

Ultimately, Gary chose to resign his credentials in good standing. In part, this decision stemmed from a conviction that he simply could no longer go along with admonishments imposed by district leaders which he perceived to be increasingly out of touch and protectionistic. Yet he describes his experience after resignation as even more painful.

> Even though I resigned with my credentials in "good standing," I've been iced out. Even from volunteering. I'm not even allowed to help at a summer camp! It's very clear that I've been blacklisted, and there is no communication. When I made a call to find out why I couldn't serve as a volunteer, I discovered that [the district leadership] had all been talking about me behind my back. "We decided you might want some time away from doing ministry," is what they said.
>
> I was told all of the conversations [leading up to my choice to resign] were confidential. So why is this happening? Now nobody will call me. Nobody will be my friend. It's clear that [all of those years] of service don't matter.[56]

This kind of marginalization is another expression of indifference and features prominently within the research sample; in many cases the fear of marginalization is as impactful as the act itself. Throughout the study, participants described being marginalized as an informal consequence to the expression of dissent: refusing to "take" abuse, refusing to keep quiet about concerns, or refusing to uphold unofficial expectations. In each case, marginalization was experienced by powerless clergy in circumstances where there were no grounds for discipline or official sanction according to the by-laws.

> I had publicly asked for help [while pastoring a very difficult church], so now I was on the list of "complaining pastors" and I couldn't get another job. Well, I tried to apply. I couldn't get interviews. In those days only the

---

56. Condensed from interview transcript.

> superintendent had the names of open churches, and what the district superintendent thinks of you is what determines if you get your résumé put in places. So, I got in more trouble for sending my résumés out directly. He felt that I went behind his back.
>
> So I was "frozen out," and isolated from my community. I was "blacklisted." I never had another pastoral opportunity until one of my childhood friends was elected as the new district superintendent. I've served faithfully for more than twenty-years since. What does that tell you?[57]

During the initial screening of participants for this study, the researcher encountered significant pushback from the central PAOC clergy base, who expressed that most allegations of abuse of power within the PAOC are "baseless" because the recipients of abusive behaviour are themselves far from innocent.[58] Essentially, these advocates alleged that those who have been mistreated "deserve" what has been done to them. (This victim blaming persists despite the availability of established procedures and by-laws that can be used to discipline credential holders who have indeed breached ethical or moral standards.) Within this sample, thirteen participants reported twenty-three distinct instances of marginalization; for eleven of those participants, no grounds for discipline existed in any form whatsoever, and nor were they ever the subject of disciplinary inquiry. For the other two participants, the threat of a disciplinary action was used against them, but it was introduced in a manner entirely outside of the official procedures established in the PAOC by-laws as a way to coerce compliance through fear; in these cases, marginalization also followed.

NDAs and Cover-Up Schemes

Cover-up schemes (which can include NDAs), demonstrate another dimension of indifference in their active attempt to silence the weaker party. Mila was the target of serious misconduct by a

57. Interview transcript S1P7. Edited for confidentiality.
58. Private source.

district leader; after collecting evidence and presenting the same to the DE, she was offered a financial settlement in exchange for an NDA.[59] The DE made no mention of any counter-investigation, nor the manner in which she brought evidence of the misconduct. Nonetheless, Mila, not the leader in question, became the villain (both privately and publicly) in the aftermath. Her district superintendent's particular concern was that in coming forward about her experience, she had "made us look bad. You made the [PAOC] look bad."[60] An insider to this event was also interviewed as part of this study, and they reported being severed from their role without warning or cause approximately six months after this event but shortly after voicing their dissent over Mila's treatment. Notably, their severance package (and future employment references) required the signing of an NDA that excluded them from sharing their knowledge of what had happened to Mila.

Winston, a lead pastor with over twenty-five years of service in the PAOC, describes a similar dynamic in his district; he raised a request for a copy of a report frequently cited in a significant policy decision being led by the district superintendent, noting that this report had never been published or released to the constituency. When his initial request for the report was ignored, he continued to press the issue. Despite the requirement that the DE respond to all official correspondence, his written requests went ignored for over a year, without even an acknowledgment of receipt. When a DE member finally spoke with Winston, on condition of confidentiality, he revealed the DE had been instructed to "keep [their] mouth shut,"[61] as there had indeed been a breach of internal protocol, which the request for the report had brought to light. Despite this, Winston was both publicly and privately reprimanded for being divisive in his ongoing request for information. He reflects, "Nobody's answering and they don't like [that I am]

---

59. The evidence included witness statements, email documentation, and audio recordings that demonstrated bullying, threats, manipulation, and lying (among other things).

60. Interview transcript.

61. Interview transcript.

asking the question. I thought we were a transparent organization . . . but information is power, right?"[62]

Hearing concerns and grievances, and responding appropriately, is essential in the creation of a valuing environment. Both Winston and Mila's experiences are examples of something quite opposite: a willful indifference bolstered by authoritarian tactics to marginalize a complainant. These are deliberate means of devaluing clergy within the PAOC. As one of the consistent themes emerging in the data is the attempt, by those in power, to control public narratives (rather than hearing, acknowledging, and responding in good faith to issues raised), this issue is indicative of a systemic problem that requires further study. It is telling that at the time of writing, there are no known instances of public institutional apology to clergy for these, or any other known, instances of abuse of power.

INEQUALITY

Steed defined "inequality" as a dishonouring of a person's humanity which includes unfair (or inequitable) treatment and systemic disrespect (for example, failing to honour and acknowledge a person's expertise professionally), in addition to acts of sexism, racism, generally berating comments, and other diminishing acts perpetrated by a supervisor.[63] These behaviours, whether intentional or not, result in members of the organization feeling like they are "not worth very much,"[64] especially in comparison to others who don't suffer these experiences.

---

62. Interview transcript.
63. Steed, *Smart Leadership*, 88.
64. Steed, *Smart Leadership*, 88.

Power in Practice

Ranking Common Experiences of Inequality

The following table provides a ranked list of coded experiences of inequality, common across the sample, following the same conventions as table 2.1.

TABLE 2.2 Common Experiences of Inequality

EXPERIENCES OF INEQUALITY (CODES AND PREVALENCE)			
Local Church Experiences		**PAOC/Systemic Experiences**	
Experiences of indifference that occurred specifically within a local church context (e.g., church staff interactions)		Experiences of indifference that occurred beyond the local church context (e.g., district and national interactions)	
CODE	RANK	CODE	RANK
Labour Complaints	1	**Sexism**	1
The experience of inequitable workplace conditions, including violations of legal employment standards and employer breaches of the employment contract		The experience of inequitable treatment solely on the basis of sex; also includes limitations for opportunity and advancement as well as reduced pay for the same work	
Favouritism	2	**Favouritism**	2
The experience of inequality due to the non-meritorious favouring of a person with whom the director has a personal relationship with; includes nepotism.		The experience of inequality due to the non-meritorious favouring of a person with whom the director has a personal relationship with; includes nepotism	
Exploitation	3	**Role-Based Discrimination**	3
The experience of being systematically taken advantage of, whether on the basis of ignorance or via direct means such as coercion and manipulation		The experience of inequitable treatment solely on the basis of role, for example, treating credential holders of equal tenure and education discriminatively based on their respective roles of lead pastor vs. non-lead pastor	

FINDINGS

Berating Comments The experience of being targeted or singled out from the group and diminished instead of corrected; also includes public and private belittling via inappropriate comparison to others	4	**Labour Complaints** The experience of inequitable workplace conditions, including violations of legal employment standards and employer breaches of the employment contract	4
Sexism The experience of inequitable treatment solely on the basis of sex; also includes limitations for opportunity and advancement as well as reduced pay for the same work	5	**Exploitation** The experience of being targeted or singled out from the group and diminished instead of corrected; also includes public and private belittling via inappropriate comparison to others	5
Racism The experience of inequitable treatment solely on the basis of race; also includes limitations for opportunity and advancement as well as reduced pay for the same work	6	**Berating Comments** The experience of being subjected to comments by an employer that are not intended to discipline or correct but only to diminish and belittle	6
		Racism The experience of inequitable treatment solely on the basis of race; also includes limitations for opportunity and advancement as well as reduced pay for the same work	7

Of particular note in this category is the sheer volume of labour complaints; no less than nineteen participants cited this as a significant experience within their local church context. These complaints speak to the very heart of Steed's definition of inequality: participants described excessive workloads, unpaid hours, toxic working conditions, breaches of their employment contract, and being manipulated by their supervisors to accept unwelcome changes to their working agreements. Some examples include:

POWER IN PRACTICE

1. Excessive Hours, No Overtime Pay

At his last church, Wayne was required to be present in the office from 9 a.m. to 5 p.m., Monday to Friday, and participate in services on Sundays, in addition to leading midweek programs three evenings per week. He averaged sixty-four hours of work per week. His employer also required him to continue his theological education "in his free time" (a condition of employment). In the province where Wayne was employed, he must agree in writing to work beyond forty-eight hours, and be provided overtime pay.[65] This is an employer responsibility, and these rights cannot be waived.[66] Further, Wayne cannot be penalized or chastised for

---

65. The legislation that requires written agreements for work beyond forty-eight hours is to enforce an employee's legal right to refuse all scheduling beyond a forty-eight-hour workweek.

66. While each province has its own rules for overtime pay, this particular scenario runs afoul of labour laws in all provincial jurisdictions (see Mehta, "What Are the Overtime Rules").

While church-based employers in some provinces, such as Ontario, have claimed that because religious leaders are an excluded class in the Employment Standards Act (ESA), the scenarios given as examples within this section are entirely legal, regardless of how unfair they may seem. However, upon consultation with an agent from the Ontario Ministry of Labour, the researcher was able to determine that only sacred duties (such as administering church ordinances) are exempt from overtime pay. In Ontario, all "regular" work by clergy, such as administration and program preparation and execution, is subject to the full provisions of the ESA, including overtime pay after forty-four hours of work (there is an exception made for managerial work, which is defined as exclusively overseeing other employees; thus a lead pastor may not be covered by this statute, although their subordinates most certainly would). The right of Ontario clergy to overtime pay is further established if clergy do not set their own working hours (e.g., required by a supervisor to maintain office hours during the week). This very issue was decided in court in Kashruth Council of Canada v. Rand (2011) when the Ontario Labour Relations Board ruled in favour of two Jewish mashgichim, noting that, while their work was religious in nature, due to their status as supervised employees (who did not set their own schedule) the Employment Standards Act (including right to overtime pay) applied to them in full.

As noted by John Pellowe, CEO of the Canadian Centre for Christian Charities, in general, despite the legal requirement to meet these standards, Christian employers (including churches) have "counted on the pastor not going to the courts to sue fellow believers" when these rights are violated, rather than simply

FINDINGS

asking questions about the employment standards in his province, however when bringing up his hours and workload, he was chastised to be "grateful" for a pastoral job. He commented, "The church was working me to death but then criticizing me for being fatigued."[67] As noted, Wayne chose not to renew his credentials and no longer pastors in the PAOC.[68]

2. Excessive Workload

When another pastor on staff was terminated, Greg was asked to temporarily assume additional responsibilities while maintaining his regular workload. There was no increase in pay or other compensation. When the church hired a new pastor, they built a new portfolio for this individual and never relieved Greg of his "temporary" responsibilities. After months had passed, he approached his lead pastor and spoke candidly: "I am being crushed. I'm drowning, I need help."[69] He explained the negative impact of the workload on his health and to his family. His lead pastor responded by saying, "This is how we stretch you as a leader."[70] He felt his only options were to continue to work in excess of seventy hours per week or resign and look for a new job. Greg resigned from his role, subsequently resigned his credentials, and no longer pastors in the PAOC.[71]

3. Unpaid Hours and Intimidation

When Cynthia was interviewed, she was told her part-time pastoral role would be compensated at nineteen hours per week. "Some weeks you'll work a bit more, but others you'll work less. It balances out." Cynthia noted that over two years, there were many weeks she worked more but never a single week she worked less.

---

abiding by the established codes (Pellowe, "How Christian Is My Ministry?," para. 5).

67. Interview transcript.
68. Summarized from field notes.
69. Interview transcript.
70. Interview transcript.
71. Summarized from field notes.

When this extra work was required for weeks on end, she would inform the lead pastor that she had used all of her paid hours, but he nonetheless insisted that she was required to attend special meetings and events. When another pastor resigned, she was informed (not asked) that her responsibilities would now include covering that job, despite no increase in her paid hours. Cynthia was now expected to be available five days per week, in addition to Sundays. Her escalating requests for consideration (full-time pay for full-time hours, or a reduction in expectations) were eventually met with intimidation and threats regarding her reputation and ultimately her future within the denomination (her pastor claimed to be well connected and influential). Cynthia ultimately resigned both her role and her credentials and no longer pastors in the PAOC.[72]

4. Contract Breach and Forced Volunteerism

Maggie objected three times (including once in writing) to taking on the additional responsibilities formerly fulfilled by a part-time employee who had resigned; she repeatedly expressed that she could not manage these responsibilities in addition to her already full-time pastoral role. Her objections were not only ignored, but her job description was amended without her consent. Maggie was upset but unaware that this is a violation of labour law. Feeling crushed by the workload, Maggie's breaking point came when the church also required her to "volunteer" for an extra five to ten hours of ministry per week and attend various off-hour prayer meetings, even if they fell on her day off. Exhausted to the point of illness, she ultimately resigned her job upon the advice of her physician; she also chose not to renew her credentials due to the lack of support that she experienced from her district office over a one-year period leading up to her burnout. Maggie no longer pastors in the PAOC.[73]

---

72. Summarized from field notes.
73. Summarized from field notes.

FINDINGS

5. Pay Withheld, Time Off Denied

Excited for the opportunity, Joseph departed from Bible college before graduating from his program following a successful interview for a pastoral position at a church in another province. He then made a significant relocation. Certain he could complete his studies at a distance, Joseph looked forward to gaining pastoral experience while studying. Upon arrival, the lead pastor suggested that Joseph had misunderstood their arrangement: the parsonage he was promised was merely a bedroom in someone else's home, and his pay was set at a mere $150 per week until he "proved himself faithful." He put his education on hold and tried to win the approval of the lead pastor by putting in full-time hours. After three months, rather than a raise in pay, he was chided for only working fifty hours per week and told to do better. After two years without vacation, and unable to make payments on his student loans (due to his meager income), Joseph reached a breaking point. He requested time off to visit his parents in the light of serious physical symptoms of ill health. When his request was denied, Joseph resigned and was subsequently accused of failing to "submit to those placed in authority over you."[74] The long-term impact to Joseph's physical health from this season of ministry lingers to this day.[75]

The Impact of Workplace Exploitation

In trying to explain how egregious abuses of employment standards have impacted her life, Emily shared this perspective:

> We couldn't go to our leaders and set boundaries, because the whole workplace culture at the church was that we are all here to "put ministry first." My pastor said that ministry was supposed to be our whole lives. I was working 82 hours a week, and they just pointed out that my contract had never listed a specific "number of hours." We were just expected to get the job done, no matter

74. Interview transcript.
75. Summarized from field notes.

what. I had very little time off, and on days that I was "off" there was the expectation of constant communication by email or text. It affected me mentally, emotionally, and spiritually. The reason I stayed is because I was young and naive. My pastor told me that my "success" [in this church] would set me up for life, and that no other pastor would give me these same opportunities.[76]

Excessive hours and unrealistic job-descriptions have a direct impact on a person's well-being; they also play a significant role in the cycle of powerlessness. Both are reasons that legal standards exist to protect employees. Cheryl Forbes notes, "We could rephrase 'barefoot, hungry, and pregnant' to read 'keep them poorly paid, eager and over-worked,'"[77] a sentiment that echoes the reality participants frequently cited: exhausted and financially desperate, they were simply unable to stand up to an aggressive and difficult supervisor. Participants also expressed that their generosity and willingness to go the extra mile was frequently abused and manipulated. Labour complaints from former employees at PAOC district offices are similar: excessive unpaid hours, lack of lieu time following busy seasons, and on occasion, the requirement to use personal funds and vacation time to attend required functions.

Other reports of inappropriate working conditions include incidents such as being directed to disregard safeguarding policies (specifically the Plan to Protect protocols required by the PAOC),[78] being mandated to preach on short notice as a "test,"[79] and even an

76. Condensed from Interview transcript.

77. Forbes, *Religion of Power*, 72. While speaking specifically to the issue of sexism, Forbes nonetheless clearly identifies the role that economic exploitation plays in keeping a demographic of people locked into a cycle of powerlessness.

78. This direction, given by a lead pastor, was in direct contradiction to specific college training the youth pastor had received on the subject. The youth pastor was subsequently belittled by his supervisor (who claimed to be a true "expert" on safeguarding) and threatened with termination if he did not yield to the direction.

79. This member of the clergy was called at home on a Saturday night and given less than twelve hours to prepare for the next day's service. The supervisor later disclosed this was part of a calculated strategy to "test" their abilities.

instance of a co-worker wiping bodily fluids onto their colleague "as a joke," which subsequently went unaddressed. Each of these incidents represents an assault on human dignity that resulted in a sense of being "lesser."

Sexism in the PAOC

Inequality is perhaps most visible in the frequent accounts of systemic sexism that emerged in the research.[80] A pattern of discrimination against female pastors, specifically in regard to the accessibility of mentors, support, and opportunity is noted. As recently as 2018, Cynthia sought to meet with a district leader to discuss the poor working conditions she was experiencing,[81] but was instead relegated to meet with an office administrator. She explained why this happened:

> It's because I am a female, and that [district leader] doesn't meet with females. It was a boy's club. I don't think I [ever] talked to [my district leader] one-on-one the entire time [I was in that district], and I don't know if what I shared was ever passed on, because nothing was ever done to help me.[82]

Samantha, a pastor with more than two decades of experience, shared that she continues to experience discrimination, even after the "PAOC Statement of Affirmation Regarding the Equality of Men and Women in Leadership" was released in 2018: "I spoke at an event, one that many people I know have spoken at before. But for some reason when I spoke, the district leaders wouldn't eat a meal with me. Hospitality was off-limits, because I'm a woman, and they are all men."[83] Other women reported direct discrimination, in the form of derogatory and discouraging comments they

---

80. Sexism is ranked as the number-one systemic issue.
81. Cynthia's complaint included serious allegations of unpaid hours and willful intimidation.
82. Summarized from interview transcript.
83. Summarized from field notes.

received over the course of their time in ministry. Some are shared here:[84]

> Do you really think this career is appropriate for a woman?
> —*Assistant district superintendent to a female pastor in their district (ca. 2000)*

> If you think you have a calling on your life, when it's truly your husband who does, you're like the wife of the pilot that thinks she can fly a plane. You will wreck his ministry and everything around you.
> —*International missions worker to female pastor applying as a global worker (ca. 2003)*

> You had better make sure you're putting out for your husband. . . . I think you should be planning a sex vacation for your husband.
> —*District executive member (same individual, multiple statements) to a female conference speaker (ca. 2008–10)*

> So, you'll be attending [event]? Would you be willing to lead the ladies devotional that's taking place while the men are in their meetings?
> —*Proxy request to a female lead pastor, originating with the district superintendent (ca. 2014)*

> Wow. I didn't know we ordained women.
> —*Lead pastor to a female pastor, following her ordination service (ca. 2016)*

> Our district superintendent hates women.
> —*District employee to a female credential holder, as explanation for her lack of opportunities (ca. 2018)*

> The way you carry yourself as a wife and a woman is repulsive. Stop overshadowing your husband.
> —*District executive member to a female lead pastor candidate (ca. 2020)*

---

84. Direct quotes from interview transcripts. Unattributed for confidentiality.

FINDINGS

The clarity with which each of these women was able to recall such hurtful words is deeply sobering; a moment frozen in their minds in which their worth and value were so clearly diminished, not just by another Christian, but by another member of the clergy. Those who have chosen to retain their credentials and persevere in the PAOC describe themselves as ministering while still wounded. One woman remarked, "I spent three months lying in my bed, crying, holding by Bible. I understand why people leave the ministry."[85]

Indifference as an Aggravating Factor

Of course, no organization is free of bad behaviour; but valuing environments are created when reports such as these are met with empathy and action. As already noted, prompt and appropriate responses to complaints by clergy over mistreatment appear to be absent in the PAOC; those in the sample who did report these experiences of inequality found either indifference or, as the next section outlines, retaliation and emotional violence.

INDIGNITY

While indifference ignores and inequality dishonours, indignity is particularly severe in that it contains an embedded violence: it invades.[86] Steed notes that while indignity may appear as "overt workplace bullying . . . or strong arm tactics," it always includes "the violation of sacred space that is the essence of violence."[87] In the ecclesial space, teachings on submission and hierarchy play a significant role in the way individuals process such violations.

Theological teaching on submission and hierarchy were cited in the experiences of indignity for fourteen of the twenty-five participants. Despite being clergy themselves (and, arguably,

---

85. Interview transcript S1P1.
86. Steed, *Smart Leadership*, 88.
87. Steed, *Smart Leadership*, 88–89.

possessing some degree of spiritual authority in their roles), the impact of being "invaded" was nonetheless consistent with the experiences common to most victims of spiritual abuse, as characterized in Maria's story:[88]

> I've received a lot of formal and informal instruction that said, "Submit to your [spiritual] authority." That's it; over and over and over and over again. In the church world where I grew up, it was all about submission, and all about hierarchy, and knowing your role, and not stepping outside of that. And so, I didn't even know that I had "rights," or that I could stand up to somebody who was doing something wrong. Because every time I would try, I would get my hand slapped.
>
> So when the person who was my spiritual authority [abused their power], and lied, and then lied to cover the lies, I was crushed. I said to myself, "I don't think I'm going to call myself a Christian ever again." I felt so disgusted by it. My stomach would turn, because I had associated the people who claim to follow Jesus and represent him with who God is.
>
> If you're asking me to be completely honest, I don't feel like I trust God [anymore]. And I think that's because I always had this idea that "as long as I'm faithful, I can trust that God will take care of me, and that he'll see me through . . ." But [in that season] I felt like everyone in my community of faith had turned their back on me. I still feel like I'm a fraction of the person that I was.[89]

In cases of spiritual abuse, participants often struggle due to a conflation of spiritual leaders with God himself. If anything, the impact is further amplified for clergy who are bullied by those who claim both spiritual and temporal authority in their lives.[90] Teach-

---

88. For a description of common outcomes following spiritual abuse, see Langberg, *Redeeming Power*, 126–29.

89. Condensed from interview transcript.

90. The duality of role for an empowered clergy member who exercises both spiritual leadership (as the pastor) while maintaining supervisory functions (as

ing on hierarchy and submission within the ecclesial community must take into account the capacity with which this teaching can be so easily exploited, lest its teachers find they have nurtured a gross violation of Christian ethics. Ross Hastings sheds light on how teaching on authority, especially within the pastoral context, ought to function:

> Understanding ministry in the light of Jesus and the Triune God we serve makes us see ourselves as collaborators, complementary to each other, rather than competitors. Jesus transforms our relationships in every realm, including in the teams where synergistic function is the goal . . . within the Trinity there are functions that do involve authority/submission, which are best spoken of not as subordination but the submission of equals.[91]

Broadly, the codes which describe experiences of indignity represent the antithesis of Hastings prescription.

Ranking Common Experiences of Indignity

The following table provides a ranked list of coded experiences of indignity, common across the sample, following the same conventions as tables 2.1 and 2.2.

---

the employer) creates a significant power differential that goes even beyond the observations of dual-role relations theory described in the literature, which describes the experience of the spiritually abused as experiences where "the follower is confused by the growing costs of the interaction, but wants to be 'good,' wants God's blessing, and strives to maintain the relationship despite increasing inner conflict" (F. Watts et al., "Unhealthy Religion," 70).

91. Hastings, *Pastoral Ethics*, 289–90.

TABLE 2.3 Common Experiences of Indignity

EXPERIENCES OF INDIGNITY (CODES AND PREVALENCE)			
Local Church Experiences Experiences of indifference that occurred specifically within a local church context (e.g., church staff interactions)		**PAOC/Systemic Experiences** Experiences of indifference that occurred beyond the local church context (e.g., district and national interactions)	
CODE	RANK	CODE	RANK
Supervisor Misconduct The experience of being violated by the unreasonable and unprofessional acts of a direct supervisor, where authority is abused to facilitate misconduct[92]	1	**Retaliation** The experience of being attacked or deliberately harmed after reporting or standing up to misconduct[93]	1
Retaliation The experience of being attacked or deliberately harmed after reporting or standing up to misconduct	2	**Fear of Retaliation** The credible fear of being attacked or harmed if one were to report or stand up to misconduct	2

92. This may include specific boundary violations (such as the inappropriate foray into one's personal life) or using legitimate functions, such as meetings, for illegitimate purposes such as intimidation or sexual harassment, or any other listed code. Note that supervisor misconduct often overlaps with other coded experiences but does not always. For example, retaliation can be an example of direct supervisor misconduct if, after becoming aware that an employee filed a WorkSafe complaint, an employer schedules their subordinate for multiple mandatory meetings that are thinly veiled excuses for hours of berating comments. Likewise retaliation that takes the form of indirect sabotage of future opportunities through blacklisting would not, in this chart, be coded as supervisor misconduct; while this certainly is an example of misconduct, this specific code is meant to catalogue instances of direct, not indirect, experiences of indignity.

93. It is important to note that "retaliation" does not include reasonable and legitimate disciplinary action; rather it describes harm unjustly inflicted upon an individual for reporting wrongdoing or resisting abuse.

FINDINGS

Intimidation The experience of actual or attempted coercion by a supervisor through direct or veiled threats	3	**Discreditation** The experience of losing credibility due to deliberate actions of reputational sabotage, either directly or subtly (e.g., casting doubt; spreading rumours)	3
Manipulation The experience of being persuaded through indirect means, including attempts to produce negative emotions (e.g., guilt, fear, etc.) or periphery pressure (e.g., financial impact to family members) to control behaviour	4	**Lying and Misleading** An experiencing of harm due to deliberately false or misleading statements of a person in power	4
Discreditation The experience of losing credibility due to deliberate actions of reputational sabotage, either directly or subtly (e.g., casting doubt; spreading rumours)	5	**Coercive Control** Experiencing a loss of agency or autonomy outside the workplace due to a person's aggressive behaviour or patterns which may include threats, humiliation, and manipulation	5
Fraud Experiencing harm due to illegal falsification of records or deliberate factual misrepresentation by a person in power to gain advantage, legally or economically	6	**Ambushed/ Breach of Process** The experience of being deliberately caught off guard and denied proper process in a disciplinary matter, also includes policy and by-law violations	6
Ambushed/Breach of Process The experience of being deliberately caught off guard and denied proper process in a disciplinary matter, also includes policy and by-law violations	7	**Intimidation** The experience of actual or attempted coercion by a supervisor through direct or veiled threats	7

Lying & Misleading	8	Breach of Confidentiality	8
An experiencing of harm due to deliberately false or misleading statements of a person in power		The experience of having protected or privileged information shared inappropriately and/or without consent, including violations of the Privacy Act	
Illegal Dismissal	9	**Criminal Conduct**	9
The experience of being dismissed for an unlawful reason, including protected grounds, as specified in the Human Rights Code		The experience of damage due to conduct described as an offence in the criminal code of Canada	
Sexual Harassment	10	**Sexual Harassment**	10
The experience of unwanted and inappropriate sexual remarks or gestures in the workplace		The experience of unwanted and inappropriate sexual remarks or gestures in the workplace	
Public Humiliation	11	**Other Misconduct**	11
The experience of being deliberately singled out for no legitimate purpose other than to be shamed, ridiculed, and diminished by others		Forms of complex misconduct that don't fall within other categories	
Breach of Confidentiality	12		
The experience of having protected or privileged information shared inappropriately and/or without consent, including violations of the Privacy Act			

In each case, the experiences coded in this category describe acts that wholly invade the sacred space of an individual, ultimately resulting in significant damage: emotional, spiritual, or economic. When asked to describe the impacts of experiences coded in this category, participants shared statements such as these:[94]

---

94. Taken from field notes and interview transcripts. Unassociated with other pseudonyms to maintain confidentiality.

FINDINGS

I stepped away from pastoral leadership and I haven't looked back. I am taking a break from pastoral work because of this experience. I wish I could say I haven't been affected, but I have.
—*Former PAOC pastor, five-plus years of experience*

All church experiences are stripped of any value for me now. We can't go. Knowing what's behind the veil, I can't sit there.
—*Former PAOC pastor, ten-plus years of experience*

I feel like I don't trust God anymore. It's not that God is bad, but these institutions ruin it. I get why people leave the church. People's lives are ripped apart by these behaviours.
—*Former PAOC pastor, fifteen-plus years of experience*

It devastated my physical health, which is now a long-term struggle. My doctor told me that this was a stress response to what was happening to me [in that situation].
—*Current PAOC pastor, ten-plus years of experience*

It was traumatic. Simple as that. And that trauma has affected how I lead others. It brings a fear to assert any kind of authority. You're afraid of being perceived to be like them. You're afraid because you ask yourself, "What if I'm abusing my power too?"
—*Current PAOC pastor, fifteen-plus years of experience*

I used to pray like a warrior conqueror. Now I pray Job prayers. "Lord, don't let me die in this pit." I had to live in David's prayer that season. All I could say was "Father, why have you forsaken me?"
—*Current PAOC pastor, twenty-plus years of experience*

Indignity as Personal Violation

Among participants who left ministry in the PAOC, the experience of indignity at the hand of a spiritual leader was especially devastating. It is important to call this misuse of power what it truly is: abuse. Experiences of indignity are violent invasions, with a lasting personal devastation. In some cases, research participants shared their experience for the first time, having never spoken out due to a fear of retaliation. In other cases, participants reported having exhausted every means of redress available to them but ultimately experiencing overwhelming indifference. The researcher finds it incumbent to include multiple examples, at length, within this section to illustrate the severity and proliferation of this abuse.

1. Bullying in the Local Church

> I didn't know why we were going to meet, but my lead pastor ripped me a new one that day. He said that I was a terrible leader and my best days in ministry were behind me. I tried to speak up, but he cut me off, saying things like "How dare you challenge my ideas on youth ministry. I wrote the book on youth ministry!" Yeah, he yelled. A lot. It was a verbal beating. He literally stood over me and berated me. It seemed like forever. He told me explicitly: "I can ruin you." I was totally intimidated.[95]

2. Inappropriate Conversations in the Local Church

> My lead pastor was weirdly obsessed with attractive high-school girls who were popular and kept trying to pressure me to spend more energy on them to grow my ministry. He always said I needed to go after the popular and attractive kids, because that's how he did church leadership as well. We butted heads often because I didn't think this was appropriate. But there were lots of things like that. One time he asked the male staff members, "Hey, if your spouse died, who would you shack up with?" I didn't answer. It just felt so inappropriate.[96]

---

95. Condensed from interview transcript S3P1.
96. Condensed from interview transcript S3P4.

FINDINGS

3. Humiliation and Threats in the Local Church

> He often yelled at me in public, a red-faced angry kind of spectacle. And in private, he threatened to fire me four times. No paperwork though. No HR documentation. No constructive criticism or performance improvement plan. Just threats and walking on eggshells. He would get upset with me because my wife didn't volunteer more, or because a last-minute project he wanted to do wasn't possible. Then he'd pull me into my office and say things like "I've talked about you with other people—a lot of credential holders in our district don't think highly of you." It was awful, but I needed the income to support my family.[97]

Each of these three credential holders reported these incidents to their district leadership; in each case no action was taken. Predictably, when incidents like these are reported, the most common response is the statement that the district has no authority over the relationship between lead and staff pastors.

Ambush and Collusion

While Emily was pastoring in the PAOC, her spouse was undergoing significant treatment related to a health crisis. One summer afternoon she received an unexpected call from another credential holder, an individual who also served on the DE. With no forewarning, he insisted she meet with him that day to discuss an urgent but confidential matter. No other information was given, and she reluctantly found childcare in order to oblige the request.

To Emily's surprise, the DE member was not alone when she arrived; she was introduced to other credential holders in attendance, and promptly informed of an allegation of personal misconduct. Emily described her reaction as stunned. "I [couldn't] even put a sentence together, " she said. The surprise tribunal presented allegations characterized by facts grossly out of context and

---

97. Condensed from interview transcript S1P6.

outright falsehoods; but whenever she attempted to provide an explanation, she was denied the opportunity to speak freely.

"I'm stuttering through [my response]," she noted, "[and he] puts his hand up and said, 'I'm going to stop you . . .'" The DE member proceeded to interrogate her, insisting on binary answers to statements riddled with half-truths. Overwhelmed and afraid, Emily was finally told she could refute the allegations, but if she did, they would be made public, and she would be suspended from her job while a full investigation into her private life was conducted. She was then given a second option: she could write a confession and resign from her pastoral role, thus quietly avoiding the ordinary proceedings prescribed in the PAOC constitution and by-laws.

At no point in the process was Emily provided a copy of the by-laws (which do not allow for this sort of informal hearing), nor was she given the opportunity to seek council or to confer with her employer directly (despite the demand that she resign from her job). Rather, she was told she needed to make a decision, alone, before leaving the meeting.

> I immediately thought of my husband. There was no way he would get through a public controversy in his present state of health. And they pressured me, they told me I had to decide before I left the room. So I protected my family the only way I knew how. I signed a paper saying that I would not contest the allegations, and I agreed to resign.[98]

She would later discover that the allegations brought to her attention that day had been made almost six months earlier and that a covert "investigation" had been taking place without her knowledge all this time (another clear violation of the by-laws). When Emily returned home after the meeting, debriefing the encounter and its immediate fallout with her family, she realized she had made a huge mistake: she was innocent of the allegation against her but had made a false confession out of fear. To make matters even worse, the public announcement given at her church

---

98. Condensed from interview transcript.

the following Sunday declared she had been terminated for misconduct, which was not what she agreed to at all.

"People thought I had had an affair, or had acted inappropriately with a minor," she explained. After the announcement was made, she approached the district superintendent to explain the coercive circumstances around her confession, rescind her statement, and ask for help restoring her reputation. He replied, "What's done is done," and was unwilling to provide an opportunity for redress. Instead, he insisted she participate in the clergy restoration program.

Emily's experience is a case study on indignity inflicted by an institution. This was grotesque violation: secretly investigated, blindsided by allegations, intimidated, denied due process, shamed, and ultimately isolated.

> I was told I couldn't talk to anyone at my church anymore. All of these people in my life were suddenly ripped out. I was told I needed to get permission just to continue my relationships with my friends.[99]

Far from being a series of missteps or mistakes, this type of experience was intentionally orchestrated. It represents a blatant abuse of power on behalf of the employer (who first received the allegation), the district superintendent (who authorized the covert investigation and subsequent intervention), and the DE (who sidestepped due process with an agenda driven by a predetermination of guilt).

Emily trusted that, as a credential holder, she would be afforded the protection of policies described in the PAOC by-laws, and that as a Christian she would be afforded the dignity of dialogue if there were concerns with her personal ethics or morality. Unfortunately, this blatant disregard the process set out in the PAOC constitution and by-laws is not unique to Emily's situation. Within the research sample, disregard for process was relatively common.[100]

---

99. Condensed from field notes.

100. This type of sidestepping takes multiple forms, whether signaled by

Power in Practice

The Use of Fear to Silence

In addition to issues of indifference that have already been outlined, the data revealed that fear of retaliation is a significant factor which enables abuse of power to go unreported, and therefore unchallenged. Once again, the perspectives of participants speak powerfully to this reality:[101]

> Institutional loyalty is a requirement for promotion in the PAOC. It's literally an "old boys club": a small group of men who have power and influence to decide and control what happens. So, I went outside the PAOC for help because I had no other choice; but I was further ostracized for that. I think it actually changed the outcome of my situation. There are people more upset that I went outside than they are with what happened to me. But "dealing with things in house" only works for those with power in that house.[102]
> —*Identity withheld*

> I knew if I approached the district, it was [career] suicide.
> —*Identity withheld*

---

statements such as "the process technically requires [stipulation], however, it would save us all a lot of time and process if we could just [proposed solution]" or as pressure, the way Maria experienced: "No one would take action, despite the evidence. And they really encouraged me not to file a formal complaint" (field notes). In both cases, the by-laws that exist are disregarded when convenient.

101. Taken from field notes and interview transcripts. Unassociated with other pseudonyms to maintain confidentiality.

102. This view, that perhaps the worst thing a Christian can do is take a matter before authorities outside the church, is common within the evangelical tradition. Books such as Albert Poirier's *Peacemaking Pastor* use pejoratives to discourage critical evaluation of when it may be most appropriate for Christians to engage civil authorities (219). Casting unforgiveness and outside intervention as sins far greater than initial offenses (108–9), Poirier makes no distinction between abuses of power and ordinary conflicts between believers, applying an inappropriately simplistic model across the board (179–81). One must not underestimate the influence of these types of resources and the philosophies behind them.

Findings

I would affirm that there is a very real fear of retaliation in the PAOC. The cost of reporting is huge. Even if those in power are held accountable, you'll be marginalized and discredited for being disloyal because you came forward.
—*Identity withheld*

My district superintendent had this line that "The PAOC is like the mafia." It terrified me and proved to be true. If you're not loyal, everyone will know. You have to show that you can take abuse in order to get on the mafia's good side.
—*Identity withheld*

I tried to get help, but nobody would. Everyone just passes the buck. One of the general officers asked, "Are you sure you want to continue? There will be an impact on you, your job and reputation if we approach that leader about this." They did everything they could to discourage me from proceeding and that's when I realized that we probably don't hear about 80 percent of the actual issues in the PAOC because people are afraid of losing their jobs.
—*Identity withheld*

I didn't feel safe to file a complaint in the PAOC or even with WorkSafe because my pastor knew everyone. His political connections meant there was no way I could take any action. I knew the board trusted him, and that my complaint would never be validated or taken seriously. He was on the district executive so I couldn't go to my superintendent for help either.
—*Identity withheld*

What he was doing was wrong, but I was genuinely concerned about my reputation. He always talks about all the people he knows, and I'm concerned what he might say about me. The way things are insinuated, you get the message. I felt like I would get in big trouble if I were talk to the district about what was going on.
—*Identity withheld*

I couldn't approach the district or anyone else for help about these situations because of the "honour code" that you don't undermine your lead pastor, and you don't complain. Whatever you say to the district superintendent could be used against you.
—*Identity withheld*

Hell no! I know that if I reach out to the district superintendent or the National Office for help with this situation, I will be labeled a "complainer." And I'll lose ministry opportunities. To continue on, I've had to be a good soldier and refuse to tell the truth about what happened. Otherwise, I'll be iced out.
—*Identity withheld*

There is no place to heal or seek help without being perceived as a troublemaker. If you talk to National Office, they say they can't do anything anyway. The risk of reaching out for help anywhere else is too high—I would look like a gossip and risk my future. If I shared what happened to me, I would be the one who is disciplined for gossip, because it's always the credential holder who "has a problem" and "needs therapy."
—*Identity withheld*

Not once did I have someone who was my advocate; when you're dealing with a credential holder that's further up in the hierarchy, you're told that you're dealing with "God's anointed." So, when they're involved, and the problem is with them, you will never have anyone to help you.
—*Identity withheld*

Retaliation

Far from being an urban legend, the fear of retaliation shared by the participants in this study appears by all indicators to be rooted in substantial evidence, with several participants sharing the impact of retaliation when they took action that was discouraged by empowered clergy:

FINDINGS

So my spouse had a job offer from another Christian organization. And it was suddenly rescinded because one of the district officers made a proactive phone call to them. My husband wasn't involved in the ministry, and nobody at the district was listed as a reference for him. They blatantly meddled after I took action against them.
—*Identity withheld*

I tried to get another job. I was so close, and then it came crashing down. The recruiter wouldn't give me a reason, just that he had spoken to the district superintendent. That's when I realized that I had been blacklisted for speaking out. He was telling people lies about me.
—*Identity withheld*

A few years ago, we were in the US. I had a meeting with a leader from another denomination about an opportunity. The first thing this leader said was that he ran into my district superintendent at a conference the week before, and my superintendent told him that my family was going through a lot and that I was in counselling. "Your superintendent said he met with your counsellors because you're really making life hard for [acquaintances] of his," he shared. A total breach of confidentiality. I was in counselling over a personal matter while a credential holder, his friend, was being investigated by the PAOC for serious misconduct. Totally inappropriate.
—*Identity withheld*

Across the sample, a clear pattern was demonstrated: in the case of power differentials, when clergy with less power speak out against clergy with more power (due to alleged misbehaviour), the result was always one of the following scenarios:

1. The subordinate clergy is informed there is no help available for them, and subsequently marginalized (as if tainted by the controversy). The subordinate clergy is initially believed, but the alleged abuser actively misleads an investigative body made up of acquaintances. There is minimal scrutiny, no

action is taken, and the subordinate is severely discredited or marginalized.

2. The subordinate is believed, and an investigation verifies the legitimacy of their allegation. Action may be taken.[103] While technically vindicated, the subordinate clergy is informally labeled a "troublemaker" and marginalized from future opportunities as if tainted by the controversy.

There were no cases where reported incidents of indignity, inflicted by clergy with more power than their own, were appropriately investigated with the complainant afforded some degree of protection from retaliatory action. Thus, there appears to be little incentive for credential holders to come forward and name any bad behaviour that they observe.

In some cases, lying and misleading goes beyond common ethics and enters the realm of fraud, extortion or other behaviour characterized as criminal. This illegal behaviour must be explored separately.

A SPECIAL NOTE ON ILLEGAL BEHAVIOUR

It must be noted that allegations of behaviour that are illegal, on some level, run throughout multiple narratives and categories, and have already been noted: employment law violations,[104] various forms of harassment, discrimination on protected grounds,[105] or failure to protect employees who experienced harassment within the workplace. For these issues to persist within the ecclesial structure is, of course, especially, troubling. This section specifically

---

103. To say "action was taken" may be misleading. While there are several incidents where offending clergy were significantly disciplined or dismissed, none of those consequences was a direct result of a complainant's verified report of misconduct; rather, those dismissals were the result of subsequent and unrelated violations more than one year later.

104. As noted, accounts of extended workweeks, unpaid hours, and constructive dismissal were common in the sample.

105. Specific instances of filtering résumés for reasons of gender and race have been noted.

Findings

means to highlight behaviour that, when reasonably described, is likely to be punishable by a judicial body. Descriptions of experiences that likely meets these qualifications are coded as indicated in table 2.4.

Ranking Common Experiences of Illegal Behaviour

The following table provides a ranked list of coded experiences of illegal behaviour, common across the sample, following the same conventions as tables 2.1, 2.2, and 2.3.

TABLE 2.4 Common Experiences of Illegal Behaviour

ILLEGAL ACTIVITY (CODES AND PREVALENCE)			
Local Church Experiences		**PAOC/Systemic Experiences**	
Experiences of indifference that occurred specifically within a local church context (e.g., church staff interactions)		Experiences of indifference that occurred beyond the local church context (e.g., district and national interactions)	
CODE	RANK	CODE	RANK
Noncriminal Law Violation	1	**Human Rights Violation**	1
Incidents elsewhere categorized that specifically relate to the violation of common law, labour law or other relevant codes. Examples in the data include breach of contract and employment standards violations.		Incidents elsewhere categorized that specifically relate to the violation of the Human Rights Code. Examples in the data include discrimination based on race or sex, and harassment.	
Human Rights Violation	2	**Criminal Law Violation**	2
Incidents elsewhere categorized that specifically relate to the violation of the Human Rights Code. Examples in the data include discrimination based on race or sex and harassment.		Incidents elsewhere categorized that specifically relate to the violation of criminal law. One example in the data: extortion.	

Criminal Law Violation	3		
Incidents elsewhere categorized that specifically relate to the violation of criminal law. One example in the data: fraud.			

As previously noted, experiences that appear to be violations of common law or employment law were quite common within the sample within the local church context. Unlike alleged violations of criminal law, the threat of punitive action for these acts rests solely on an employee's willingness to take legal action upon themselves, a burden that clergy seem unwilling to bear at present. In contrast, violations of the Human Rights Code (which cover issues of discrimination and harassment on protected grounds) are less frequent, however often more serious, especially when patterns of behaviour are clear.[106]

Alleged criminal law violations, while most rare, are especially serious. These codes represent experiences that, when described, appear reasonably likely to be indictable as a criminal offence in Canada: namely, an instance of fraud (in the local context) and criminal extortion (in the systemic context). When potential criminal conduct was identified in interviews, it always appeared as a reactionary development; an escalation after other means to control a situation did not yield the desired results.

Criminal Extortion[107]

In one example, a member of the clergy reported being extorted into resigning their job and signing an NDA while under threat of personal harm, specifically in the form of reputational damage

---

106. One participant was able to demonstrate clear patterns of repetitive racial harassment in the local context; two others were able to demonstrate a pattern of discriminatory exclusion based on sex, including filtering résumés. Another female described a pattern of sexually inappropriate and demeaning comments by a well-known senior member of the clergy.

107. See Government of Canada, "Criminal Code."

and resultant financial ruin through a blackmail scheme.[108] The alleged perpetrator was stated to have admitted this manipulation scheme to a third party who subsequently disclosed the scheme to the victim. This course of action allegedly took place following the supervising clergy's unsuccessful search for legitimate grounds to terminate this employee. As the victim of this scheme was unable to afford legal services, the fear for their livelihood superseded their willingness to fight.

> I knew I didn't do anything wrong, but they said they had all this evidence. Even though I would win [a PAOC] disciplinary hearing, it wouldn't matter, because they're so powerful and I wouldn't be able to get a job after that.[109]

This participant thus signed an NDA, which prohibits them from sharing this experience publicly or disclosing other evidence of misconduct.

Fraud

In another instance, a member of the clergy experienced sudden health complications at work. They were advised by their employer to appeal to their physician for the note appropriate for a disability claim. Only after the paperwork was filed and medical treatment began did the leader discover the organization's disability insurance benefits policy had lapsed.

In an ill-advised scheme to make good on the commitment made, the supervisor allegedly revised the employer portion of the federal paperwork to reflect a "laid off" status, without informing the disabled pastor. Upon receiving notice of this change by mail, the disabled pastor questioned their employer, who admitted the lapsed insurance policy and confided that the organization had determined to top up the standard unemployment benefit

---

108. The perpetrator of this act had claimed (to the victim) to have damning physical evidence of inappropriate behaviour, with fabricated props to enhance the ruse.

109. Source withheld for confidentiality reasons.

(in cash and "under the table"), provided that this member of the clergy would go along with the scheme.[110] Uncomfortable with this fraudulent arrangement, he refused, and was subsequently asked to resign and sign a NDA in exchange for severance.[111]

The Role of NDAs

The role that NDAs play in these types of situations are especially noteworthy. Originally designed to protect trade secrets from competitors, it is difficult to discern if there is any legitimate use for an NDA by a Christian organization. Certainly, weaponizing NDAs in order to safeguard a personal or institutional reputation in the face of misconduct is unethical, and considering that a standard confidentiality clause in an employment contract is sufficient to provide for safeguarding organizational information or other ordinary data, the justification for NDA use is especially unclear. As it stands, there is no guideline within the PAOC on how and when an NDA may be used. Even in this relatively small sample, the indiscriminate use of NDAs appears to be a problem that requires a response.

CHAPTER CONCLUSION

Overall, the evidence that experiences of inequality, indignity, and even illegal behaviour have gone unchecked is significant; further, the impact of indifference toward clergy who have experienced

---

110. In addition to violating the Employment Insurance Act (No. 38 (1), c.23 S.C.), and the Criminal Code of Canada (No. 380 (1), C-46 R.S.C.), these undocumented payments would likely also have violated the legislation that governs financial rules for registered charities. There would also have been nonmonetary penalties for both the employer and the employee for engaging in this scheme, as detailed in Service Canada, *Employment Insurance and Fraud*. As it stands, knowingly falsifying the ROE is an offence that can carry significant consequences in its own right.

111. Federal unemployment benefits also require the recipient to testify biweekly that they are looking for work; as the pastor was receiving medical care, he was also being asked to lie about this status.

Findings

these things has been costly. The narratives that have emerged in this research are ultimately indicative of a culture where abuse of power has proceeded unchecked, and likely remains quite prevalent. The stark absence of reporting structures or whistleblower policies play a key role in the experiences emerging from the sample group, as does the fear of retaliation embedded within the ministerial culture. In this light, the risk that clergy who fall victim to abuses of power will continue to be silenced is especially troubling.

Nonetheless, the data also presents an opportunity for significant theological reflection on the embedded operant theology that has underpinned these experiences, as well as broader questions about power, anthropology, and the reification of Christian ethics. These subjects will be engaged more fully in chapter 4, following a review of the relevant literature.

3

Literature Review

A NOTE ON THE ABSENCE OF SPECIFIC LITERATURE

While literature on the general nature and philosophy of power is abundant (and reflective of varying Christian theological perspectives), the same cannot be said for literature concerning the role of power within inter-clergy relationships. Serious academic work has been undertaken regarding the nature of ecclesial structure and the church's relationship with power, but in almost every available case these works reflect on the relationship between the church and the broader world; an examination of external, not internal, dynamics. Conversely while a considerable body of literature has emerged around the issue of abuse of power within the church over the past twenty years, this literature focuses almost exclusively on the relationship between clergy and congregants, and not on the interpersonal dynamics that exist between members of the clergy themselves.[1]

---

1. The two notable exceptions here are Chuck DeGroat, *When Narcissism Comes to Church* (which takes a broad and inclusive view of the problem of narcissism, including the impact of narcissistic behaviour on other members of the clergy); and Paul Beasley-Murray, *Power for God's Sake*, which will be discussed separately.

LITERATURE REVIEW

In the absence of a large body of literature related to the primary question of this research project, I have engaged in a transdisciplinary review of significant work that intersects with, and at times runs adjacent to, the focus of study. The significance of this study is, in part, to fill a gap in knowledge, and by appealing to formal theology outside of the PAOC (the voice of the academy proper) a more informed theological dialogue between the four voices can take place in chapter 4. Great care has been taken to locate material that has specific relevance to the focus and emerging themes of this project. Specifically, this chapter presents a summary of significant literature that speaks to the overlapping themes of power, Christian ethics, theological anthropology, the abuse of power (specifically within an ecclesial context), and an approach to reflective praxis concerning the same. Take note that this is not an exhaustive list of literature but rather a spotlight on key material that fills the gaps in the dialogue. For a complete list of material engaged, refer to the bibliography.

A PHILOSOPHY AND THEOLOGY OF POWER FOR THE CHURCH

Without failing to acknowledge the significance of Michel Foucault, Max Weber, John Locke, Karl Marx, or Thomas Hobbes in the quest to define "power" (and qualify the nature of its use), it is the exploration of mediated power, specifically within the framework of Christian faith, that emerges as the urgent task in this study. How Christians think about (or ought to think about) power in the light of their faith presents a significant lens through which the research data must be analyzed.[2] Engaging the work of Richard Niebuhr and Jürgen Moltmann, Stephen Sykes summarizes three perspectives in *Power and Christian Theology* that are especially helpful in arriving at some kind of model from which to proceed.

---

2. This is, in some ways, an attempt to discover the normative theological voice, which, while always mediated by one or more of the other voices, must speak authoritatively to questions posed about power, humanity, and ethics.

Power in Practice

First, an ordinary, "popular" and imprecise definition of power is appropriate when engaging the subject. Sykes argues that the historical discourse around power, even cross-culturally, is essentially dialectic; thus, an attempt to capture an entirely precise definition of power may result in something that is effectively misleading.[3] There are many ways of exercising power, and definitions claiming universality may be unable to address the dynamic means through which power is expressed in an unanticipated context. As such, Sykes argues that theologians must pay close attention to the popular definitions of power emerging within their culture, as these reflect the social reality of how power is used in the real world that Christians must inhabit. Thus, simple definitions, such as "power is the ability to influence,"[4] though not comprehensive, can be useful.

Second, Sykes speaks consistently to the Christian perspective on the origin of power; that all power exercised by human beings is, in fact, an exercise of mediated power that finds its ultimate source in God. This carries significant implications, not least of which that human beings are divinely accountable for their uses of power, both small and great.

Third, Sykes asserts that a comprehensive Christian theology of power must differentiate itself from the work of secular philosophers by becoming uniquely centred on the cross of Christ, and that it is the mortification of power that comprises the definitive contribution of the Christian faith to the wider discourse.[5] While Sykes makes a formidable case, cruciformity in isolation presents a narrow theology of power which could benefit from the added dimensionality assumed by Moltmann, namely that "the primal power of life, [is that] which Paul calls in Romans 8:11

---

3. Sykes, *Power and Christian Theology*, 5–7. Sykes points out that the dialectic of Greek ἐξουσία (the freedom to do a thing) versus δύναμις (the ability to do a thing), the Roman *auctoritas* (informal social power) versus *potestas* (legal power), and the German *macht* (power) versus *herrschaft* (domination) all demonstrate the nature of the discourse around power across culture and history.

4. Nye, "Changing Nature of Power," 1.

5. Sykes, *Power and Christian Theology*, 16.

Literature Review

the 'indwelling' resurrection Spirit of God."[6] Indeed, God's power is made visible in the cross, the resurrection, and in the work of the Holy Spirit; and all three are necessary to comprehend the fundamental reversals that a Christian ethic of power, emerging from the New Testament, uniquely imposes upon secular models of power.[7] Sykes's framework thus contributes to the formation of a normative metric for evaluating the ongoing exercise of power within the church by approaching the question of whether power observed (for instance, in the research data) is exercised "Christianly": in meekness, humility, and in service to others.

As the exercise of power can take many forms (and arriving at a clear description of those forms is functionally necessary), the metric emerging from Sykes's work benefits from a psychosocial perspective on the types of human power, and here Diane Langberg's descriptions are most helpful.[8] These dynamic expressions of human power, for both Langberg and Sykes, serve as evidence of God's divine plan for human agency, which must not be impinged, even as it is held accountable.[9]

A brief exploration of contemporary evangelical literature on power (which speaks to the tradition within which this study is located) finds that definitions of power, when given, are generally qualified within the context of a careful (and sometimes wary) acknowledgment of the immense capacity for harm when that power is misused. For example, Katelyn Beaty follows up an excellent working definition of power ("the innate human ability to

---

6. Moltmann-Wendel and Moltmann, "To Believe with All Your Senses," 5.

7. See John 13:1–7; Matt 28:5–10; Acts 2:22–38.

8. Langberg, *Redeeming Power*, 8–10. Langberg lists the types of power as: verbal power (the use of words to influence), emotional power (the capacity to influence another's emotions), physical power (the ability to exert strength), charisma (socially dynamic influence), specialized knowledge (the capacity to control based on providing or withholding information), authority (formal or informal leadership), economic power (the use of financial means to influence), spiritual power (the engagement of the mystical to exert influence), and community power (the collective influence of a group of people on an individual).

9. Langberg, *Redeeming Power*, 10.

steward the world, to glorify God and bless creation and fellow image bearers")[10] with an immediate acknowledgment that with such glorious potential comes the real possibility of misuse. Viewed holistically, warnings such as these may be taken as an important indicator that the term "power" is simply not a neutral term within the evangelical tradition. *Power* (at least from a Christian perspective) is the potential of an individual to bless or curse God's creation, including other human beings; by the volume of books on the subject, it appears the latter which has become a source of growing popular concern.[11]

Steven Ogden provides a helpful explanation as to why Christian literature and dialogue on the nature of power may follow this pattern so closely: there is a uniquely heightened potential for corruption and power abuse within the Christian context.[12] Ogden argues that the great power reversals that the teachings of Christ present create opportunities for exploitation by those whose personal models of power have not yet been converted.

> In terms of theorization, there is a cluster of concepts like forgiveness, grace, charity, and obedience, which are representative of Christian piety in particular, and ecclesial discourse in general, which are open to exploitation. As

---

10. Beaty, *Celebrities for Jesus*, 69.

11. The 2024 publication of such titles as Fitch, *Reckoning with Power: Why the Church Fails When It's on the Wrong Side of Power*; Griffith, *Forgiveness After Trauma: A Path to Find Healing and Empowerment*; Brooks, *Holy Ghosted: Spiritual Anxiety, Religious Trauma, and the Language of Abuse*; Stankorb, *Disobedient Women: How a Small Group of Faithful Women Exposed Abuse, Brought Down Powerful Pastors, and Ignited an Evangelical Reckoning*; and Byrd, *The Hope in Our Scars: Finding the Bride of Christ in the Underground of Disillusionment* demonstrates the prominence of this conversation within the evangelical subculture.

12. Ogden argues that this has long been an historical reality and that the church has often rewarded parishioner compliance while sacralizing a sovereign view of their own authority (*Church, Authority, and Foucault*, 28, 51). While this practice has been, at times, discouraged (e.g., Gregory the Great, *Pastoral Rule*), it has also been grotesquely promoted (e.g., Giles of Rome, *On Ecclesial Power*); and as the Doctrine Commission of the Church of England so aptly points out, discussions on power peak within culture whenever powerlessness or authoritarian action become especially visible (*Being Human*, 33).

such, this book contends that the concept of obedience is a major factor. For example, sovereign power exploits the axiom that good sheep are obedient, and as obedient sheep they should forgive others, just as Jesus the good shepherd commanded (Matt 18:21–22). Moreover, the culture of obedience goes hand in hand with a culture of secrecy. In fact, it is indispensable to its operation.[13]

Ogden further asserts that when Christians fail to redeem the models of power they inherit from the world (whether personally or institutionally), there is an even greater susceptibility for interpersonal harm than that which exists in other contexts. A critical question emerges here: To what extent does a Christian theology of power foster a practical awareness and a deeper understanding of the heightened capacity for power abuse within the Christian framework?

In this light, it is pertinent to reflect just as much on the absence of systems and structures designed to mitigate the abuse of power as it is to reflect on any instances of abuse themselves. Philosophies of power, whether conceptual or applied, must therefore take into account both the objects and subjects of power as being theologically significant. To this end, we turn to the discussion of human beings themselves.

THEOLOGICAL ANTHROPOLOGY AND VOCATION

The work of the Doctrine Commission of the Church of England in *Being Human: A Christian Understanding of Personhood* presents a wide and helpful summary of the Christian tradition in relation to this subject that is concise enough to be wielded within the scope of this project.[14] The Doctrine Commission asserts that

---

13. Ogden, *Church, Authority, and Foucault*, 8. Ogden's comments are especially poignant in the light of Poirier's assertions to this effect (Poirier, *Peacemaking Pastor*, 108–9).

14. For brevity's sake, only the discussion on personhood and power will be referenced here, though there is much more that could be added via reflection on the sections entitled "Money," "Sex," and "Time."

humanity is foremost defined by its relationship to God, "the Almighty": made in his image, mediating his power.[15] This requires that Christian reflections on the nature of power take into account the ordinary human experience where agency is most commonly expressed. The Doctrine Commission asserts that human vocation is actually rooted in one's identity as an empowered being who, ultimately, exercises agency that is entrusted, not independently generated.[16]

Being Human concludes, with Ogden and Sykes, that this is indeed the basis for an ethic of human accountability: if the power humans exercise is extrinsic, not inherent, then the human use of power must be morally accountable to its originator. To this end, the literature points toward an examination of the ways that one's use of power is experienced by others, and how those experiences align with the Christian vision for humanity. This expands the dimensionality of both Sykes's and Ogden's call for an audit of expressions of power within the Christian context, both individually and institutionally.[17]

Finally, because the person of Jesus Christ is central to a Christian understanding of human identity, the Doctrine Commission suggests that any Christian conversation on power, including its impact on other people, must also include a reflection on the incarnation, passion and resurrection of Christ.[18] Thus, as previously noted (but now more clearly defined), the crucified and resurrected Christ presents a paradox that leads to a radical

---

15. Doctrine Commission, *Being Human*, 32, 45. The Doctrine Commission's view of humanity is complementary to underlying perspectives presented by Sykes, Langberg, and Ogden.

16. Doctrine Commission, *Being Human*, 50.

17. Doctrine Commission, *Being Human*, 40, 49. The Doctrine Commission takes great care to acknowledge where the misuse of ecclesial power has caused tremendous harm, in addition to providing a framework for critique. Further, it pays specific attention to the expression of power as patriarchy (a cultural and sociological reality), domination (the capacity to impose one's will), authority (the claim of legitimacy), sign (the implied relationship between a display of power and the will of God), and malignancy (the ability of power to corrupt those who wield it) (33–38).

18. Doctrine Commission, *Being Human*, 45–46.

redefinition of power which critiques all other modalities, while yet providing a unique contribution in itself: power as an expression of love.[19]

THE ABUSE OF POWER WITHIN THE CHURCH

In the light of the call for Christians to embrace an ethic of power that is rooted in love and service to others, the expanding volume of contemporary literature about the misuse of power by Christian leaders is especially disheartening. This growing body of work provides an heuristic for the nature of the abuse of power within the ecclesial space, in addition to serving as lagging evidence of a systemic problem. Over the course of this research, four particular texts emerged with special relevance to the findings in chapter 2. As each of them describes and diagnoses different ways power is misused in the church, they collectively provide a map within which to place the data collected in this study. As the descriptions they contain often bear a striking resemblance to the firsthand accounts in chapter 2, they are especially helpful in interpreting those experiences.

Mullen: Something's Not Right

Mullen's work emerges from the analysis of approximately one thousand cases of clergy abuse between 2015 and 2020, and is especially helpful as it effectively distinguishes "abuse" from other forms of unpleasant behaviour and benign personality conflict. Mullen defines the *abuse of power* as "any action that takes power from another in an attempt to use them" and notes that this behaviour does not have to express itself physically in order to constitute abuse: psychological, financial, and verbal forms of abuse inflict tremendous harm on their victims.[20]

---

19. Doctrine Commission, *Being Human*, 47.
20. Mullen, *Something's Not Right*, 3.

Whether clergy possess formal power (such as a position), or informal power (such as social influence derived from long-standing friendships with other power brokers), the mere existence of a power differential provides a structural opportunity to abuse a subordinate. Of course, not every person in a position of power abuses those they lead; so Mullen turns toward understanding which factors may increase the likelihood of exploitation.[21]

First, abusive behaviour can be a form of unhealthy self-medication; if a leader is "empty, narcissistic, and hungry, they'll likely feverishly quest for legitimacy and meaning, collecting audiences, platforms, awards, and luxuries to justify the position and their title."[22] Second, abusive behaviour may be rooted in the goal of protection and preservation of a role or institution (particularly if the potential for reputational damage threatens the stability of either).[23] Third, abusive behaviour may stem from an inculcated sense of tribal loyalty; for example, when a clergy member's personal security or advancement are felt to be linked directly to their ability to "do what must be done" (for the so-called good of the tribe), they may be willing to perpetrate acts they would otherwise classify as wrong.[24]

Mullen concludes that behaviours for facilitating abuse follow a predictable pattern; there is a "playbook of tactics" that is consistent among abusive leaders within Christian institutions.[25] Summarized, the abuser's "playbook" consists of:

---

21. Mullen cautions against trying to diagnose motivation (noting that even among those who do perpetuate abuse, the motivation may be unclear) and insists that communities should focus on identifying toxic behaviour (*Something's Not Right*, 106). Notwithstanding, Mullen does provides three general motivations for abusive behaviour as a means to contextualize the types of behaviours most often observed.

22. Mullen, *Something's Not Right*, 25.

23. Mullen, *Something's Not Right*, 23.

24. Mullen, *Something's Not Right*, 29.

25. Mullen, *Something's Not Right*, 29.

Literature Review

1. **Flattery:** Developing a culture of constant praise where sincere and necessary criticism are culturally disallowed.[26]
2. **Lavish favours:** Creating dependence in order to exercise greater control and influence (for example, low base salaries with generous, albeit unpredictable, bonuses at the leader's disposal).[27]
3. **Rushed vulnerability:** Calculated moments of oversharing in order to manipulate sympathy or give others a false a sense of being a confidante.[28]
4. **Disfiguring another's identity:** Creating sustained and inappropriate pressure for conformity to the abuser's style and values until independence is diminished (this is a form of grooming).[29]
5. **Multifaceted disrespect:** Using public and private humiliation in order to erode strength and weaken resolve, allowing for greater control.[30]
6. **Creating anxiety:** Creating chaos or imposing of arbitrary rules with severe consequences in order to destabilize a person's ability to make decisions (this dismantles their agency).[31]
7. **Isolation techniques:** Attempts to separate a person from other relationships, institutional support, or outside knowledge, which may involve punishing or intimidating those who engage outside the organization without the leader's permission.[32]

---

26. Mullen, *Something's Not Right*, 38.
27. Mullen, *Something's Not Right*, 41.
28. Mullen, *Something's Not Right*, 45.
29. Mullen, *Something's Not Right*, 56.
30. Mullen, *Something's Not Right*, 59.
31. Mullen, *Something's Not Right*, 62.
32. Mullen, *Something's Not Right*, 72–77.

8. **Direct intimidation:** The use of either implied or overt threats to silence someone and keep them from confiding their experiences in others.[33]

9. **Reversal tactics:** The sudden adoption of a victim stance, accompanied by a plea for compassion and mercy, as a means of manipulation through guilt when other tactics are ineffective.[34]

DeGroat: When Narcissism Comes to Church

Whereas Mullen seeks to identify the general characteristics of power abuse within the church, DeGroat suggests that the root cause of this abuse may be diagnosable narcissism, both individual and systemic.

> Sadly, narcissism in the clergy is under studied. When I did my doctoral work over a decade ago, I discovered vast resources on pastoral well-being, including studies on burnout, addiction, and depression. I found popular articles on narcissistic leadership but an absence of studies on the prevalence of narcissism.... In my own work, which includes fifteen years of psychological testing among pastors, the vast majority of ministerial candidates test on the spectrum of Cluster B DSM-V personality disorders, which feature narcissistic traits most prominently. The rates are even higher among church planters.[35]

While DeGroat speaks broadly to the experiences of parishioners who have been negatively impacted by abusive Christian leaders, it is of particular significance that the pretext for his research was a personal experience of clergy-to-clergy abuse at the hands of a narcissistic pastor.[36]

---

33. Mullen, *Something's Not Right*, 85.
34. Mullen, *Something's Not Right*, 89–97.
35. DeGroat, *When Narcissism Comes to Church*, 19.
36. DeGroat, *When Narcissism Comes to Church*, 14.

LITERATURE REVIEW

DeGroat identifies the five environmental characteristics of communities where narcissistic leaders remain generally unchallenged in their abuse of others as follows:

1. They are hierarchical structures, with a male-dominant and well-networked elite group of leaders.

2. They contain personality-driven cultures, where charismatic individuals are given automatic preferential standing and others are formally or informally subordinated.

3. They employ shame-based systems where confidence is informally equated with holiness and spiritual authority. Members are diminished or marginalized if they question the validity or inspiration of elevated leaders.

4. They are loyalty-oriented systems, where honest feedback and meaningful accountability are absent, and critique is perceived as an attack on the institution (and thus punished accordingly).

5. They are organized as a success-driven enterprise, where "results" are deemed to be the highest indicator of God's favour and approval. For example, leaders will be protected from scrutiny as long as there are reports of people "getting saved," church growth, or well-attended meetings.[37]

Further, DeGroat notes that Christian denominations with nontraditional ordination processes, where "young leaders are snatched up and deployed without proper training or soul formation, simply because they've been successful in other arenas,"[38] suffer even higher rates of abuse within their ranks.[39] The limited

---

37. DeGroat, *When Narcissism Comes to Church*, 21–23. DeGroat uses the term *malignant narcissism* as a clinical description of those who land on the edge of the narcissism scale as judged solely by their behaviours, not as a pejorative label of individuals; the term is likewise is used throughout this project in the same context.

38. DeGroat, *When Narcissism Comes to Church*, 21.

39. DeGroat references post-denominational churches that do not require a master of divinity to be completed within the denominational seminary nor a long, structured, postgraduate apprenticeship process.

vetting of untrained young adults who are invited into the bright lights of a ministry platform creates a much greater potentiality of both being abused by a narcissistic senior leader and of becoming one of the same. DeGroat notes that while narcissism can be an individual psychological diagnosis, it should also be considered as a pathological description of a system that has taken on and internalized over-arching narcissistic traits.

Besides providing clear descriptions of narcissistic behaviour that are useful in categorizing the actions described within the sample, DeGroat also provides a helpful framework for understanding the cause: the recipe is unhealed shame and brokenness, which must be addressed both carefully and compassionately.[40]

Langberg: Redeeming Power

Langberg contributes to a foundational understanding of power as she summarizes and reflects on fifty years of practice with victims of trauma.[41] Of further interest is her extensive exploration of the themes which emerged within the research data, particularly the impact of sex, race, and positional authority in abuse of power. Langberg's tenure as a psychologist and researcher is evident through her expert contextualization of these concepts and thus *Redeeming Power* provides a comprehensive overview of the use (and misuse) of power from a practical, and at times clinical, perspective.

Churches suffer a unique vulnerability to the abuse of power due to their function in mediating spiritual experience. Langberg provides a metric for an exploration of the power differentials that enable this vulnerability, while also demonstrating how members of a religious system might be complicit in the abuse of power, even if they are not the primary perpetrator. Some examples are:

---

40. DeGroat, *When Narcissism Comes to Church*, 19.
41. Langberg, *Redeeming Power*, 3–45.

Literature Review

1. **Insecure complicity:** Triggered by a sense of crisis, here members are predisposed toward reduced scrutiny of leaders, systems, and activities than they otherwise would be if not experiencing a sense of desperation.

2. **Informed complicity:** This occurs when a group of leaders derive personal benefit from their place in the organization (e.g., increased influence, social standing, financial gain, or other privileges) and would face the potential loss of these benefits if they confronted abuse.

3. **Partnering complicity:** Whenever the activities of the church, ministry, or denomination are referred to in terms of divine mission, followers (including those without power) are more likely to develop an idealistic loyalty to the organization, resulting in a willful blindness toward misconduct and a propensity to attack those perceived as threats (regardless of merit). By attacking, isolating, and discrediting would-be "threats," members feel they are preserving something uniquely special that God has created and they are a part of.

4. **Passive complicity:** When the broader spiritual community perceives that they might experience personal emotional discomfort if their institution is exposed (perhaps in the form of guilt, a crisis of belief, or loss of purpose), they are more likely to choose a willful denial that leads them toward a passive response, even in the face of significant evidence.

5. **Spiritualized complicity:** Thinking of the reputation of Christ, and how tarnished it would be if unfavourable revelations were to come to light, members of the Christian faithful may be willing to ignore credible allegations in order to cover, minimize, or even deny what they suspect to be true. These acts may be esteemed as a form of godliness that is protecting the church and ensuring that the mission of God might continue unimpeded.[42]

---

42. Langberg, *Redeeming Power*, 79–84, 132–33.

The identification of these complicity motivators is especially relevant in light of the need to explore the theme of passivity. Additionally, the comfort of cognitive dissonance that each motivator appeals to leads one to consider that allegations of power abuse between clergy might be more likely to be dismissed than if similar allegations of abuse were brought forward by a congregant (due to exacerbation of the power dynamics within inter-clergy relationships).

Of further importance to this study are the clinical insights offered on the symptoms common in persons who have endured power abuse in the church. As the most common outcomes, Langberg describes shattered relationships, experiences of isolation and marginalization, a sense of fear and shame, a loss of dignity and trust, the development of spiritual numbness, and symptoms of anxiety when engaging faith.[43] Notably, these outcomes are not commonly associated with entitled employees or those whose feelings are merely hurt through genuine misunderstandings. And while spiritual abuse is deeply traumatic, it is significantly exacerbated by experiences of indifference:

> Having been abused by someone in the system, they ran to the shepherds. Those shepherds ignored, silenced, rejected, and blamed them. The abuse of the "Christian" system multiplies exponentially the damage done by a single perpetrator.[44]

Langberg's analysis of the systems and patterns present within broad research samples provides a practical frame for the locating the experiences of this study's participants.

Blodgett: Lives Entrusted

Barbara Blodgett's *Lives Entrusted: An Ethic of Trust for Ministry* demonstrates its relevance to this project by offering a rich study on trust and Christian ethics as a backdrop for understanding

---

43. Langberg, *Redeeming Power*, 7.
44. Langberg, *Redeeming Power*, 147.

Literature Review

the relationships between clergy. For Blodgett, trust must be conceived as a verb (as opposed to a noun), and thus the act of trust is the foundational transaction in the formation of relationships.[45] The positive choice to trust is central to the capacity for relational health, both individually and institutionally. Blodgett asserts that "trust always involves risk, vulnerability, and power,"[46] and thus it must be negotiated within an informed ethical framework.

Of particular relevance to this study are Blodgett's insights on the nature and impact of lying within a relationship of trust. Citing Immanuel Kant, she argues that "physical coercion treats someone's person as a tool; lying treats someone's reason as a tool,"[47] and thus lying is an exploitation of the relationship which constitutes a form of interpersonal violence.[48] Within the Christian moral code (of which clergy are obligated to participate) bold lies and active deceptions are rarely tolerated. After all, telling overt lies is an undeniable violation of God's command, and for clergy (more than most), being caught doing so carries the risk of consequence.[49] But what of more subtly deceptive speech? Blodgett asserts that a different form of lying is not only exceptionally common among clergy but is dynamically associated with clergy who hold higher levels of institutional power:

> There are false statements that are not necessarily factually untrue but nevertheless have the effect of steering the hearer away from the truth. There are things people say without the conscious intention of deceiving others, but with so little concern for veracity that the truth often

---

45. Blodgett, *Lives Entrusted*, 2, 9–10.
46. Blodgett, *Lives Entrusted*, 2.
47. Kant, *Lectures on Ethics*, 229; as cited in Blodgett, *Lives Entrusted*, 135.
48. Blodgett, *Lives Entrusted*, 134.
49. For brevity's sake, a complete discussion of Blodgett's approach to the morality of overt lies is not given here. It is important to note that her dialogue on the subject goes well beyond overly simplified axioms and takes into account ethical dilemmas that might make lying more moral in certain circumstances, such as the preservation of life in the face of criminal violence. This truncated summation is, however, faithful to her conclusion within the context of this literary review.

> ends up being misrepresented anyway ... there are utterances meant to persuade, convince, impress, or placate the listener, in which the end becomes more important than the means. While the end may not be [overt] deception, neither is truthfulness. We could put here the growing phenomenon of "spin," to which we are all increasingly subjected. I would argue that these various categories of speech (all these variants on the lie) are as worthy of our moral attention as lying, if only because they are so prevalent.[50]

Blodgett refers to this type of talk as "bullshit" and further notes that it is the primal temptation of empowered clergy: "Defined in contrast to liars, bullshitters do not care one way or the other about the truth and deceive their listeners by pretending to be sincere and authentic."[51]

In other words, persons in position of spiritual authority may pride themselves on their technical truthfulness, all the while breaching trust via their attempts to "persuade, convince, impress, or placate," which ultimately cause relational damage comparable to the telling of overt lies. Blodgett would argue that these acts of "bullshitting" represent an important point of moral culpability.

> Because trusters are always put in some position of vulnerability vis-a-vis the people they entrust, the trust relationship always involves a differential of power.[52]

Blodgett asserts that verbalizing the capacity for harm in a trust relationship is a foundational practice in the formation of healthier systems. Within institutions where "bullshit" has disenfranchised members, this verbalization is especially necessary for the work of healing and restoration. Incorporating Onora O'Neill's framework of interpersonal accountability, an application of Blodgett's framework within the ecclesial context begins with requiring members of the clergy to actively disclose the power differentials present in their relationships and, in doing so,

---

50. Blodgett, *Lives Entrusted*, 136.
51. Blodgett, *Lives Entrusted*, 3.
52. Blodgett, *Lives Entrusted*, 22.

LITERATURE REVIEW

to invite those over whom they hold power to judge their actions accordingly.[53]

Special Mention: Power for God's Sake

Paul Beasley-Murray's *Power for God's Sake* deserves special mention as the singular work of empirical research that explores the specificity of inter-clergy relationships within the larger dynamics of ecclesial power.[54] Thus his work provides a valuable introduction to a wide range of scholars on the subject of power, including psychologists,[55] theologians,[56] sociologists,[57] and spiritual directors;[58] due to this interdisciplinarity, Beasley-Murray fosters an opportunity for a comprehensive critique of inter-clergy power dynamics that are especially relevant to this study.

Power for God's Sake frames its commentary on power and abuse in the local church within a robust exploration of the theology of power, and from there concludes that central to the problem of abuse lies a failure to identify certain uses of power as coercive or manipulative, with further failure to respond appropriately. Reflecting on his data, compiled via ministerial and congregational surveys, Beasley-Murray provides helpful insights into the question of why the abuse of power occurs and what type of action may be most appropriate to remedy such occurrences.

---

53. Blodgett, *Lives Entrusted*, 26.

54. While a great deal of his work is concerned with the use of power between clergy and congregant, Beasley-Murray both broadly and specifically includes data on inter-clergy relations (*Power for God's Sake*, 64) as well as the presence and absence of accountability structures (57).

55. Of note, Patricia Foque, Adolf Guggenbuehl-Craig, and Rollo May.

56. Insights from the likes of James Newton Poling, Martin Hengel, Cheryl Forbes, Anthony Bash, and Walter Wink add depth and context to Beasley-Murray's analysis of the data.

57. In particular, the insights of Larry C. Ingram and Bruce D. Reed.

58. Beasley-Murray's exploration of Richard Foster's and Henri Nouwen's reflections on power are significant in their own right and provide a helpful inflection point in the dialogue of the spirituality of power.

Power in Practice

While the survey data demonstrates shared perceptions among ministers and congregants that clergy are indeed accountable for their use of power on some level,[59] ancillary inquiries into the systems of accountability established within institutions were determined to provide the best indicator of the potentiality for abuse of power.[60] While an audit of an organization's power safeguards will include the review of documented systems, structures, job descriptions, and review processes,[61] the inquiry ought not be limited to published procedures or written guidelines, as these are noted to have a limited effect within systems that are philosophically informed by a perspective on spiritual leadership which conflates the exercise of power by clergy with the exercise of power by God.[62] To that end, Beasley-Murray sadly concludes that, "generally speaking, accountability appears to be a myth."[63] Practically speaking, such systems effectively preclude any meaningful accountability for misuse of power by creating a culture where abuse can actually occur within the rules of the system. As example, Beasley-Murray cites a popular seminary resource by Roy Oswald, C. Peter Wagner, and Calvin Miller:

> In his introduction to a seminary textbook, Calvin Miller declares: "If God has called you to lead, do so! All leadership is strong. Weak leadership is no leadership.... Lead with power or do not call yourself a leader." Miller then goes on throughout his book to speak of "power leadership" and "power leaders." Unfortunately such statements, unqualified, can be misleading. They can easily encourage the abuse of power.[64]

---

59. Beasley-Murray, *Power for God's Sake*, 57. The survey showed that 75 percent of clergy and 90 percent of congregations believed that clergy were held accountable by either groups or individuals.

60. Beasley-Murray, *Power for God's Sake*, 56–57.

61. Beasley-Murray, *Power for God's Sake*, 150.

62. Beasley-Murray, *Power for God's Sake*, 168–69.

63. Beasley-Murray, *Power for God's Sake*, 57.

64. Beasley-Murray, *Power for God's Sake*, 73. The citations are attributed to Calvin Miller, *The Empowered Leader*.

LITERATURE REVIEW

This observation is poignant and particularly relevant to this study. Whenever an underdeveloped theology of power is present, the likelihood leaders will never be held accountable for misuse of power is significant. As such, Beasley-Murray observes that inappropriate expressions of power, such as acts of coercion and manipulation, may continue to be perpetuated despite "even the most sincere and honest self-examination"; human frailty is no match for unhealthy cultural norms and theological poverty.[65]

Beasley-Murray arrives at a prescriptive response that can be summarized as the need for a commitment, within institutions, to define Christian leadership across all levels, as "power exercised in trust,"[66] with performance evaluations centered on qualities of gentleness, self-control, truthfulness, and selflessness, not merely church growth, financial reports, and the like.[67]

> True Christian leadership always enhances the life of others, whereas the abuse of power always leads to the destruction of others. True Christian leadership refuses to use others—whether they be individuals or churches—as stepping stones. . . . Important as are such things as competence and ability, even more important is love and sacrifice.[68]

While emphasizing the enormous potential embedded in a praxis that is theologically congruent with this ethos, Beasley-Murray also presents a warning, that the improper use of power has an equally unlimited capacity to undermine gospel work, even if the institution is otherwise entirely faithful to the Christian mission.[69]

---

65. Paul Tournier, *The Violence Inside*, as cited in Beasley-Murray, *Power for God's Sake*, 127.
66. Beasley-Murray, *Power for God's Sake*, 148.
67. Beasley-Murray, *Power for God's Sake*, 138, 155.
68. Beasley-Murray, *Power for God's Sake*, 138.
69. Beasley-Murray, *Power for God's Sake*, 141.

4

Theological Response

CHAPTER OVERVIEW

AS NOTED, THE EVIDENCE presented in chapter 2 is overwhelmingly indicative that the PAOC's concerns regarding abuse of power between clergy are not only well placed but potentially underestimated. Likewise, in light of the literature's contribution to the dialogue, it seems doubtful that the anthropological framework within the formal theology of the PAOC (as identified in chapter 1) is adequate to support the formation of a comprehensive response to issues of power abuse. However, before offering practical suggestions to remediate these deficits, (this will be the focus of chapter 5), a theological analysis must take place. Exercises in practical theology (such as this study) seek to instigate renewed praxis; in part, because the present praxis (what the four voices call the operant theology) is revealed to be inadequate. Precisely because practical theology "will take seriously the concerns, perceptions, and expressions . . . [of] the people themselves,"[1] theological inquiry must precede recommended action so that a cycle of unreflective pragmatism does not escalate the problem it seeks to solve. Rather, "theological normativity is located in Scripture

---

1. Cartledge, *Practical Theology*, 29.

THEOLOGICAL RESPONSE

and can challenge and modify the values embedded in the [present] theological praxis."[2]

Accordingly, this chapter attempts to engage the voice of normative theology as a way of critiquing, responding, and in some cases, "breaking through" espoused and operant modalities that passively preclude meaningful change. As noted in chapter 1, the operant voice of theology is present in the actions of the faith community; this chapter will undertake an analysis of the theological presuppositions observed within those actions in two sections, "Rightly Bearing God's Name" and "Imago Dei," before responding to the espoused theology of the PAOC (the voice of the institution) in a critique of Gene Edwards's book, *A Tale of Three Kings*. Finally, a renewed praxis, faithful to the theological discourse of this chapter, is presented as an alternative to the wholly pragmatic model observed in the data.

RIGHTLY BEARING GOD'S NAME

An assumption of what constitutes morality is integrated into both the formal and espoused voices of the PAOC. The standards for clergy conduct include the specific priority of leading other Christians through a faithful and holy example,[3] and thus clergy are called to be the "first-followers" of Christ as they discharge their duties.[4] Historically, Pentecostals have embraced this view of clergy, developing detailed written prescriptions related to their personal holiness standards;[5] yet Carmen Imes presents a challenge to the status quo in this regard, via a fresh exegesis of Exod 20:7 and the Sinai discourse as a whole, in *Bearing God's Name*.

Arguing that the Western Church has had an anemic understanding of what it means to "take the Lord's name in vain" (Exod

---

2. Cartledge, *Practical Theology*, 29.

3. See PAOC, "General Constitution"; PAOC, "Ministerial Code of Ethics"; Trask et al., *Pentecostal Pastor*, 106.

4. Russell, "Choosing God's Call," para. 1.

5. See Trask et al., *Pentecostal Pastor*, 105–17; Synan, *Century of the Holy Spirit*, 2–3.

20:7), Imes posits that the absence of a contextual hermeneutic surrounding the decalogue has broadly led many denominations to miss the gravity and substance of the second commandment (which absolutely insists on the right and ethical treatment of all human beings),[6] while cultivating a hyper-fixation on rules for speech as a demonstration of godliness.[7] In this light, she offers a new translation of the passage that is especially useful for understanding the connection between this commandment and the development of a biblical and theological ethic of power:

> You must not bear (or carry) the name of Yahweh, your God, in vain, for Yahweh will not hold guiltless one who bears (or carries) his name in vain.[8]

It is the significance of the "bearing" (or carrying) language that shifts the interpretation toward a poignant consideration of personal ethics. Imes points out that the peculiar language in this text is a direct reference to priestly vestments, both the medallion Aaron "bears" (or carries) on his turban (inscribed *qodesh layahweh*, which means "holy, belonging to Yahweh"),[9] and the breastplate he wears, which bears the names of the twelve tribes. Carrying the seal of the Lord identifies the bearer as both a vassal and an official representative,[10] and thus requires accurate representation in words and action. Thus, when the command is given to all of Israel (not merely the priestly class), it must be understood as an ethical imperative given to a "kingdom of priests" who bear the name of the Lord in each moment of their ordinary lives.[11]

---

6. Imes, *Bearing God's Name*, 40–43. While aware of differences in numbering the Ten Commandments across Christian tradition, Imes argues, "Do not take the Lord's name in vain" is the second commandment, based in part on the grammatical structure of the passage (*Bearing God's Name*, 45–48).

7. Imes, *Bearing God's Name*, 48–51.

8. Imes, *Bearing God's Name*, 49.

9. Imes, *Bearing God's Name*, 73.

10. Imes, *Bearing God's Name*, 50. See also Greer et al., *Behind the Scenes of the Old Testament*, 140; Pittman, "Seals and Sealings," 320–27.

11. Imes, *Bearing God's Name*, 31.

THEOLOGICAL RESPONSE

> At Sinai, Yahweh claims this nation as his very own and releases them to live out their calling. That calling is to bear Yahweh's name among the nations, that is, **to represent him well**. . . . To bear his name in vain would be to enter into this covenant relationship with him but to live no differently than the surrounding pagans.[12]

In reference to the four voices, Exod 20:7 is effectively a warning to the representatives of Yahweh to be careful that their operant theology is truthful. Considering Imes's argument (that failing to grasp this meaning sets a very low bar, reducing the command to a limited prohibition of "cursing,"[13] and that this limitation enables a religious culture permissive toward the abuse of power in the name of divine service),[14] it is incumbent that the behaviours catalogued in this study are analyzed in this light.[15]

If "rightly bearing God's name" is understood to mean a faithful representation of God's character through one's actions (especially in the exercise of spiritual power), the cumulatively alleged behaviours emerging from the narratives stand out as a catastrophic failure of holiness. One is certainly not "rightly bearing the name of God" when they are berating their staff, mandating excessive hours in violation of labour law, covering up offences, or cleverly orchestrating an ambush for a suspected violation of morality. Here, Diane Langberg's descriptions of complicity motivators (particularly partnering complicity and spiritual complicity; although informed complicity deserves a special mention due to the frequency of "passivity" in the sample) provide a psychological framework for understanding the dissonance between these actions and the base Christian morality that ought to easily preclude their commission.[16]

---

12. Imes, *Bearing God's Name*, 51, 53; emphasis added.
13. Imes, *Bearing God's Name*, 48–49.
14. Imes, *Bearing God's Name*, 49–53.
15. This makes no particular comparison between contemporary clergy and the cultic priests of the Old Testament but rather appeals to the universality of the command and the responsibility of clergy as exemplars of the faith.
16. Langberg, *Redeeming Power*, 79–84, 132–33.

Precisely because the PAOC sees its mission as particularly urgent,[17] the tolerance for abusive behaviour within the network of clergy is increased (there is an expectation that ministers will put the "mission" first). This view presumes a level of acceptable sacrifice and hardship for ministers, even if such hardship is inflicted by a fellow member of the clergy. The need for a more robust formal theological voice becomes especially apparent within this context; without an adequate theological anthropology, the age-old question of whether the end justifies the means is likely to be answered overwhelmingly in the affirmative. When this is the case, a confession of sin can be effectively disguised as the burden of leadership:

> This was a really hard decision, and we are grieved that people were hurt and disadvantaged in the process. With that being said, we had no choice. We have a mission from God and any other course of action may have jeopardized our effectiveness.[18]

While ideal circumstances are rarely seen, and there is no guarantee that the faithful and ethical use of power will always result in a freedom from anguish or loss for all involved, sanctimonious appeals to realism must not be held up as an excuse for a failure to integrate such a foundational ethic. To "rightly bear God's name" is to pursue the will of the Lord in a manner that is consistent with the way of the Lord; an ethic of power marked by cruciformity, love, and moral integrity.

IMAGO DEI

Moving toward a more comprehensive theological anthropology is thus an essential part of developing the renewed praxis. This section will explore how excessive workloads and marginalizing behaviours can be critiqued and reformed through theological reflection. While continuing with the Sinai motif, consideration will

---

17. See Luscombe, "Here to Serve," para. 3 and subtitle: "Reclaiming a Sense of Urgency to the Call of God"; Wells, "Aligned for Mission," paras. 8–9.

18. Paraphrased to protect the identity of the source.

THEOLOGICAL RESPONSE

then be given to the New Testament case against a spiritual justification for disregarding another's welfare, before articulating an anthropologically informed ethic of power in the final subsection.

The basis of this reflection is rooted in a continuation of Imes's exploration of the Sinai covenant and its anthropological implications. While acknowledging the limitedness of the PAOC's formal doctrine of humanity, the foundational premise that underlies this analysis is nonetheless intact:

> Formed in the image of God, both male and female, humankind is entrusted with the care of God's creation as faithful stewards.[19]

This belief, that human beings are formed in the image of God, sets an expectation over both how they will behave and of how they must also be treated. Such an assertion is a sharp contrast to the other ethical codes at work in the ancient world in the time of the Old Testament.

The involvement of the entirety of Israel in the covenant with God,[20] the broad scope of the law they then received,[21] and the direction in which this law "points,"[22] all indicate that the biblical ethic is uniquely permeated by an anthropocentricity unseen in the wider ancient world.[23]

> Daniel Block calls the Ten Commandments a "bill of rights." However, unlike the Bill of Rights in the US Constitution, Block points out that these ten do not focus on a person's own rights but the rights of one's neighbor. The job of every Israelite is to protect other people's freedoms. And it's done by keeping the Ten Words.[24]

19. SOET, s.v. "Creation."
20. As opposed to merely kings or priests.
21. Specifically, ethics that cover all aspects of ordinary life, not just national or ceremonial duties.
22. That is, the concern for the basic rights of all people, not merely a kingly or priestly class.
23. Imes, *Bearing God's Name*, 61–64; Provan et al., *Biblical History of Israel*, 134; Brueggemann, "God Who Gives Rest," 566.
24. Imes, *Bearing God's Name*, 53.

Seeing the decalogue as the "Bill of Other People's Rights" involves each recipient of the law recognizing the power that they possess.[25] Both corporately and individually, the power to obey or disobey is inherent to the Sinai discourse, and the objective of "Ten Words" is to direct human power toward the blessing and care of others.[26] As such, a biblical theology of power emerges in this moment that emphasizes a sense of solemn responsibility: the covenant is for everyone, and thus everyone (with whatever degree of agency they possess), is called to exercise their power in a way that protects the well-being of others. The corollary is equally true, and the use of power to harm or disadvantage, is universally prohibited.[27]

Honour the Sabbath

In this light, the reported impact to health, family and spiritual vitality among clergy who were manipulated or coerced into overwork must be taken very seriously. Variances in working week norms between the biblical era and the present can hardly account for the gross differential between the average Canadian workweek (36.9 hours)[28] and the hours reported by those in the sample group (particularly when one considers the excess with which clergy hours exceed provincial maximums and the inequity present in

---

25. Imes, *Bearing God's Name*, 53.

26. Imes, *Bearing God's Name*, 53.

27. As alluded to by both Imes and Provan, it is not merely the universality of the commandments that is unique to Israel but the provision of justice available without regard for social class, a general anomaly in the ancient world. This is thoroughly discussed by Hans Boecker (*Law and the Administration*, 53–65).

28. According to Statistics Canada for reference period Jan. 2024 (https://www150.statcan.gc.ca/t1/tbl1/en/tv.action?pid=1410021101). Notwithstanding the argument that contemporary workers labour for many more hours per year than their premodern counterparts (Riis, "Analysis of Working Hours"), the contextual issue Sabbath presents, at least according to Imes, is one of equity and well-being; the reality of social norms (e.g., rest required from normative responsibilities) impacts both.

refusing the associated overtime pay legally required).[29] Considering the geographic variance of these experiences, it appears likely unhealthy labour norms are deeply enculturated within the PAOC.

Some evidence of this is found within the customizable personnel manual for church administration, a 2016 document provided as a national administrative resource on the PAOC website. This template includes a workload model for "Pastoral Support Staff" that includes expectations of three evenings per week of ministry (at three hours per evening), availability on Saturdays as required, and entirely open-ended hours on Sundays. It further states:

- Due to the professional nature of Pastoring, hours extra prior or following set times shall be considered ministry/gratis. A general rule of hours for work and ministry will be 50 hours/week.

- One (1) day off a week, Monday to Friday, to be set by/with the Lead Pastor and Administrator.[30]

The statement that extra hours shall be considered "ministry/gratis" means that additional time (even beyond the fifty-hour model) is uncompensated and expected as a "gift" from this member of the clergy to their church. Needless to say, such employment conditions are a violation of employment standards in every Canadian jurisdiction,[31] and attempts to justify these types of conditions via a spiritualization of the particular work, (e.g., "but

---

29. The prominence and frequency of labour complaints within the sample, especially untenable and exploitive work hours, is significant and includes workweeks that reached the seventy- to eighty-hour range, with responsibilities regularly invading a singular day off. These experiences, which also included required unpaid work, are gross violations of employment standards across all jurisdictions, which, on average, legally require overtime pay beyond forty-four hours per week (see Indeed Employer Content Team, "Ontario Overtime Pay").

30. PAOC, *Personnel Policies Manual*, 11.

31. For further discussion on the claim that clergy are exempt from the protection of employment standards legislation, refer to the section on "Inequality" in ch. 2.

ministry work is service for the Lord!") should be rejected as an indicator of deep theological poverty.[32]

Returning to the Sinai discourse, it becomes quickly evident that the current praxis was formed either in ignorance or disobedience to the commandment of Sabbath (Exod 20:8), and thus a correction is required.

> Remember the Sabbath day by keeping it holy. Six days you shall labor and do all your work, but the seventh day is a sabbath to the Lord your God. On it you shall not do any work, neither you, nor your son or daughter, nor your male or female servant, nor your animals, nor any foreigner residing in your towns. (Exod 20:8–10)

Implied in this command is the assumption that some individuals, by virtue of their role or status, will have the power to influence and control the work requirements of their subordinates. While political and cultural hierarchies in the ancient Near East provided kings and masters with the privilege of rest and leisure, their subordinates and those in the lowest classes were often afforded only limited reprieve; not so under the rule of Yahweh. Building on her interpretive framework, Imes asserts that this command is intended to ensure that

> it's not just the master of the house who gets a day of rest, while everyone else waits on him. Rather, the entire household is free to participate in this rhythm of grace. . . . Sabbath is not simply ceasing from labor, but actually enjoying its results from the other six days.[33]

Sabbath recognizes God's gracious gift to all human beings: a break from labour whereby health, relationships, and deep spiritual life have room to flourish. Thus, when those with authority fail to grant rest to their subordinates, they do more than exhaust them, they deface them as human beings. The overwork of image

---

32. Namely due to the utter callousness that this perspective maintains, ignoring the devastating effect on the well-being of the clergy (and their families) upon whom these conditions are imposed.

33. Imes, *Bearing God's Name*, 54.

bearers for the building of "God's kingdom" is simply incoherent within normative biblical theology.

The application of the Sabbath command is where theological anthropology intersects with a theology of power. While an individualistic reading of Exod 20:8–11 will primarily hold each overworked member of the clergy responsible for failing to rest, a return to the "Bill of Other People's Rights" as an interpretive framework immediately holds responsible deacon boards, lead pastors, and denominational leaders for the standards of labour they tolerate, normalize, and impose upon those who serve under their leadership.

Do Not Bear False Witness

Contemporary disputes between clergy, as with any interpersonal conflict, continue to reflect today an underlying reality of the proto-Sinaitic and exodus eras: when both party's claims of truth are incompatible, the status of each individual is likely to significantly influence the outcome. Such is demonstrated within this study, where a universally favourable outcome is recorded for those in positions of power regarding all allegations of misconduct inferred in tables 2.1, 2.2, 2.3, and 2.4.[34] While a statistical analysis of probability has not been undertaken, anecdotally it seems reasonable to assume it unlikely that clergy with greater positional power or social influence were factually the victims of false accusations in every case reported.

Of further interest is the frequency with which fear of retaliation was cited as a reason misconduct was not reported, along with narratives that describe the consequence of reporting mistreatment as some form of marginalization or active discreditation.[35]

---

34. Of note, several participants noted that the PAOC takes "very seriously" allegations of financial misconduct or sexual immorality, but beyond these specific allegations, there is simply no response. Resolution 20, the amendment to add nonsexual abuses of power to the by-laws as a disqualifying moral failure, is meant to respond to this very issue.

35. The phenomenon of discrediting and marginalizing those who bring

Power in Practice

Accounts of lost friendships, abandonment by the ecclesial community, and economic hardship due to false reports of their impugned character are as raw as they are frequent within the sample. When cross-referenced with accounts of empowered clergy lying to, misleading, or (to use Blodgett's terminology) "bullshitting" the broader constituency, the Sinai discourse once again emerges as a point of significant theological reflection, particularly Exod 20:16: "You shall not give false testimony against your neighbor."

The non-anthropocentric hermeneutic (which Imes has been so diligently dismantling) might interpret this commandment primarily as a prohibition against misrepresenting the facts of a particular matter; yet the object of this imperative is not a depersonalized piece of evidence, it is a human being. In absence of a normative theological anthropology, the priority of "your neighbor" is easily de-emphasized: a poorly formed theology of power centered on personal interest does not read the decalogue as the "Bill of Other People's Rights" but rather as parameters for one's personal conduct. While subtle, a grammatical focus on the subject (instead of the object) of the commandment informs an interpretive framework that focuses intently on the technical details of a behaviour instead of God's broad intent: articulating a law that gives life.

While telling lies about inanimate facts is certainly immoral, the deep significance of bearing false witness "against your neighbor" (Exod 20:16) is in its disfiguring of their identity. The castigation and marginalization of whistleblowers is not primarily problematic because such actions impede future employment opportunities, or even because these acts signal impunity to those who are misusing power,[36] but rather because these acts bear false

---

grievances forward cannot be adequately explained as merely the natural inclination of an accused person to defend themselves, as many cases involve the systemic marginalization of a complainant by the institution as a whole (the broader ecclesial leadership that informally punishes a minister who reports mistreatment from clergy with greater power). This is further explored within this section as an example of institutional preservation.

36. By "not primarily problematic" I mean only to say that while these are significant problems in their own right (which deserve earnest consideration)

testimony about the identity of the persons themselves. This violation is further aggravated when religious jargon is used to justify it.

The prioritization of "the church" (as institution) or "the mission" (as sacred task) over human beings themselves has become a recurring theme in these analyses; by all accounts, this represents a well-intentioned but theologically problematic perspective with deep roots in the PAOC.[37] Conflating the reputation of the institution with the cause of Christ itself, clergy who marginalize and discredit whistleblowers or instigate a cover-up scheme may be

---

there exists an even greater consequence for marginalization that cannot be remediated merely by reversing these secondary impacts (e.g., appointing to gainful employment and holding the offending party accountable).

37. As context, the phrase "what is best for the Church is best for me" is emphasized within the PAOC church administration manual (Alberta and NWT District, *Church Administration Manual*, 60), a sample document from the recently archived "Church Administration Resources" repository on the PAOC website (https://web.archive.org/web/20220707125046/https://paoc.org/ministry-toolbox/church-resource-documents/church-administration). As a philosophical framework, this sample features a section meant to guide pastors who may have been wronged or mistreated in the process of exiting church employment. The manual admonishes clergy toward action that prioritizes the stability, reputation, and well-being of the local assembly, regardless of any personal harm that they might have experienced. Of course, professionally speaking, airing one's so-called "dirty laundry" as a form of revenge or self-medication is wholly inappropriate. However, the dilemma that this research highlights is the gross absence of qualifying criteria to distinguish between personal disagreements and acts of misconduct when clergy experience hurt. Evidence that subordinate clergy were expected to keep quiet or participate in cover-up schemes is found both within the research sample and in another repository template, the *Church Leadership Philosophy Manual*, which specifically requires staff pastors to "defend the Senior Pastor from unwarranted comments, slanderous remarks, *true or false accusations*, and any other form of gossip or malicious comments directed at him and members of his family" (Alberta and NWT District, *Church Leadership Philosophy Manual*, 21–22; emphasis added).

The balance of evidence suggests that this perspective ("what is best for the Church is best for me") has been used to silence and discourage clergy from reasonable actions to redress serious issues (e.g., employment law violations, discrimination, harassment, etc.). Thus, the overall impact of the "church first" philosophical framework is the de facto prioritization of institutional stability over clergy well-being, regardless of official intent.

excused as "only looking out for the best interest of the church."[38] Langberg indicts this perspective as being explicitly antithetical to the normative theological voice on the matter:

> People are sacred. Systems are not. They are only worth the people who are in them and the people they serve. And people are to be treated, whether one or many, the way Jesus Christ treated people.[39]

The engagement of Imes's hermeneutical shift (as discussed) is thus more than merely a matter of biblical study; it represents an opportunity for the transformation of the underlying praxis evident within the current operant theology. Moving from a subject-oriented to an object-oriented reading of the Sinai discourse shifts the proof of morality in each of these situations away from debates over whether the subject of the command "technically" did or did not lie, and onto whether the object of the command had their identity disfigured. As such, this framework is generative toward an evaluative awareness reflective of Beasley-Murray's assertion that "true Christian leadership always enhances the life of others, whereas the abuse of power always leads to the destruction of others,"[40] or more colloquially, it cuts through the image of ministry "success" to examine whether or not there are "bodies behind the bus"[41] and invites an anthropocentric shift reflective of normative Christian ethics.

---

38. Source withheld for confidentiality.
39. Langberg, *Redeeming Power*, 87.
40. Beasley-Murray, *Power for God's Sake*, 128.
41. This metaphor is used repeatedly in the *The Rise and Fall of Mars Hill* podcast series, a journalistic report on allegations of power abuse by Mark Driscoll, who used this phrase to describe his willingness to sacrifice ministry leaders to achieve the ultimate goals of his church. In episode 5 of the series, "The Things We Do To Women," this term is especially poignant and is used to summarize the significant spiritual and emotional damage that was inflicted on members of that church community. Due to the reach of the podcast, "bodies behind the bus" has become a symbolic metaphor of those who were used, abused, and discarded by a Christian institution. See Cosper, "Things We Do."

Theological Response
A New Testament Critique of Spiritualized Indifference

Imes's assertion that Exod 20:8–17 ought to be read as an effectual "Bill of Other People's Rights" in order to capture the significance of God's concern for the well-being of humankind finds further support in the New Testament. While much can be said about Israel's idolatry (and her resulting exile) in the generations that followed the Sinai covenant, Rikk Watts aptly points out that in the New Testament, the historical failure of Israel to recognize and respond to the anthropocentric themes in the law emerged as a significant conflict between God (in Jesus) and the religious institution. In a cross-reference of Mark 7:9–13 with Exod 20:12, Watts also concludes that a subject-oriented reading of the decalogue had led to the failure of religious leaders to apply the theological anthropology embedded in Torah.

> At issue, then, are not the ritual purity codes per se. It is instead the hypocrisy of worship (whether involving Sabbath or purity) that *meticulously observes human regulations but hard-heartedly ignores God's requirement for the welfare of people,* not least in circumventing [God's] clear command concerning parents in order to protect personal interests, [which] aggressively *denies the Torah's core orientation to glorify God by doing good and bringing life.* . . . In the midst of an intensive conflict over the nature of holiness, his opponents' hard-heartedness on this particular point of Torah more clearly than most invokes the threat of God's exilic censure.[42]

The text Watts refers to is the controversy revolving around the care of parents, as commanded by God at Sinai (Exod 20:12), that emerges in chapter 7 of Mark's Gospel:

> And [Jesus] continued, "You have a fine way of setting aside the commands of God in order to observe your own traditions! For Moses said, 'Honor your father and mother,' and, 'Anyone who curses their father or mother

---

42. R. Watts, *Gospel of Mark,* 106, 108; emphasis added.

is to be put to death.' But you say that if anyone declares that what might have been used to help their father or mother is *Corban* (that is, devoted to God)—then you no longer let them do anything for their father or mother. Thus you nullify the word of God by your tradition that you have handed down."

Corban, in facilitating a creative loophole by which support for one's parents could be redirected for the benefit the religious institution, invoked the anger of God. As it could be personally advantageous to dedicate "to the Lord's use" resources meant for the good of one's parents, this incident serves as shorthand for the critique of prioritizing personal and religious interests over faithfulness toward the care of others.[43]

As Watts notes, the issue at hand is the actual welfare of the mother and father associated to this story. To put it succinctly, Jesus' objection is that it had become religiously acceptable to disadvantage and dishonour human beings, as long as it was in done in the name of religious service; he accordingly indicts this neglect as a sin against the one in whose image humans are made.[44] While echoes of this sentiment within the New Testament are evident,[45] Jesus' alignment with an anthropocentric, object-centered reading of the decalogue is especially significant for the context of this study.

In both the Sinaitic and first-century contexts, normative theological anthropology is used as a means to calibrate (or recalibrate) base levels of tolerance for antihuman behaviour. In consideration of the prior discussions on the prioritization of religious

---

43. In his article "Vowing Away the Fifth Commandment," Jon Bailey notes that "in an age when the Temple still stood, [corban] may well have been used to dedicate property that would subsequently be given [to others] as an offering to God. Yet the previous evidence examined in this study suggests that the formula was also used to prohibit others from using something by declaring it consecrated as far as they were concerned" (Bailey, "Vowing Away the Fifth Commandment," 202).

44. Note Watts's specific notes regarding the Isaianic warnings implicit in Mark 7:10 (*Gospel of Mark*, 107).

45. Particularly the use of Mark 12:30–31 in Jas 1:27—2:26. See also Matt 23:23; Luke 10:25–37; 11:37–46.

success, the Markan discourse on corban further emphasizes what has already been established; such priorities are misguided and in actuality represent a spiritual anathema.

Moving Toward Remediation

Having established the anthropocentric focus of the theologically normative ethics emerging from Exod 20:1–17, we now turn to the task of articulating a renewed framework for the use of power within ecclesial leadership. This requires a challenge to the model of power observed within the common experiences of the sample group. As noted, the model of power observed as the operant theology in the PAOC is one where power is primarily exercised in the service of one's own agenda. While a benevolent expression of this model is no doubt pursued with great intentionality, perhaps in seeking to sanctify one's interests, the susceptibility to inappropriately conflating one's agenda with the will of God remains too real. At its worst, this model of power quickly gives way to exploitation, where others are "used" as a means to an end. This is visible within the data in multiple forms; while the vast majority of power abuse identified within the sample appears to be opportunistic, this does not diminish the devastating impact to the target. To this end, it reveals the sobering reality that "unholy power models are systems that can only produce the unholiness of the dark lord who stands behind them."[46] The model itself must be overhauled; a renewed praxis must be the goal.

Borrowing from the formal voice of the literature, this task of renewal begins with a declaration that all human power is entrusted power, originating from God, given for the service of others.[47] A truly Christian model of power affirms that the agency gifted to humanity is inextricably tied to the human vocation, with accountability embedded therein. Here, the formal voice of the PAOC could be amended as follows:

---

46. Sykes, *Power and Christian Theology*, 13.
47. Sykes, *Power and Christian Theology*, 27.

Power in Practice

> Humankind is entrusted with **power for the purpose of the care of God's creation, especially other human beings who are both the subject and object of his care in their calling** as faithful stewards.[48]

Here, holiness is not an abstract concept; rather it is relating rightly to God, humanity, creation, and ourselves.[49] "Relating rightly" is thus the formative framework that serves to engage a Christian vision for renewed interpersonal ethics, especially in the light of power differentials. In his 2014 work, *Seriously Dangerous Religion*, Iain Provan articulates this praxis in action as he describes a biblical and theological ethic for human relationships:

> The God who will not be treated as an object also demands that human beings not treat their neighbors in this way. The God who insists on being addressed as "Thou" rather than "It" also insists that mortal beings should not disregard their neighbor's personhood. The God who will not allow mortal beings to use him for their own purposes also sets limits on the human tendency to use others ... [and commands] the rejection of neighbor destroying and the embrace of neighbor keeping activities.[50]

The conviction that these two theological axes are inextricably connected provides a framework for the regulation of the exercise of power along a very particular morality; it engages self-deceptive religion by exposing interpersonal violence as abhorrent, regardless of whatever false piety attempts to disguise it.

From this vantage point, a practical metric emerges: any praxis that produces experiences of indifference, inequality, and indignity

---

48. Modified from SOET, s.v. "Creation." Additions emphasized.

49. This particular way of articulating holiness is helpful as each of these requires a theologically informed model of power and the Christian vocation in order to be successful.

50. Provan, *Seriously Dangerous Religion*, 206–7. Provan's argument (that the proper treatment of men and women, and thus the right use of power, is actually a reflection of one's right relationship with God) provides an important waypoint for an ongoing critique of theological modalities that might seek to reimagine Christian faithfulness in a more abstract form.

in human beings must be indicted as definitively un-Christian, and subsequently deconstructed.[51] Likewise this praxis positively presupposes ministerial work as the sacred trust of leading those whom God loves: human persons who bear his very image.

SUBMISSION AND ABUSE

Throughout the interviews with current and former clergy, the theme of "spiritual submission" was an accompanying presence, especially in its impact on perceptions of leadership, boundaries, grievances, and the ability to leave a toxic situation. While it cannot be overstated how significantly this dynamic affected the participants within the sample,[52] a specific aspect of the submission theme that warrants examination are the references to Gene Edwards's 1992 allegory *A Tale of Three Kings*. Whether a direct reference to the title, a literary allusion (for example, phrases such as "be a David to your Saul"[53] or "he's still God's anointed"[54]), or the experience of receiving a copy of the book from another leader, the data is indicative of a wide familiarity with Edwards's work.[55]

The popularity of this book and the surrounding folklore about the importance of submission to spiritual authority (at all costs and at all times) represents a touchstone issue for the PAOC. As such, an examination of this work of historical fiction represents an opportunity to examine the espoused theological voice of the movement in regard to power, submission, and appropriate response.

---

51. The use of the categories from ch. 2 is intentional, as this provides a greater degree of evaluative clarity than more general terminology.

52. An incapacitory effect was noted multiple times as clergy stayed in situations that were clearly unhealthy for extended durations of time. For an example, see Joseph's story in ch. 2, "Pay Withheld, Time Off Denied."

53. Interview transcript S3P1.

54. Interview transcript S1P2.

55. Notably, Edwards's work bears a striking resemblance to the tone of the replies that participants personally received from denominational leaders upon reporting mistreatment.

Power in Practice

A Misappropriated Story

Subtitled as "a study in brokenness," *A Tale of Three Kings* dramatizes the portion of King David's biography that intersects with Saul and Absalom. Presented as an Old Testament guide to leadership, the book is comprised of twenty-three short chapters and is as accessible as it is brief. Recommended as a sort of "survival guide" for young pastors who find themselves employed by a difficult lead pastor, Edwards makes no fewer than twenty references to Saul as "the Lord's anointed" and openly suggests that only God knows if a spear-throwing leader (such as the mad King Saul) may yet still be God's chosen one. Thus, he advises young leaders to diligently dodge the missiles, and above all, keep quiet, as this sample captures:

> Unlike anyone else in spear-throwing history, David did not know what to do when a spear was thrown at him. He did not throw Saul's, spears back at him. Nor did he make any spears of his own and throw them. Something was different about David. All he did was dodge. What can a man, especially a young man, do when the king decides to use him for target practice? What if the young man decides not to return the compliment?
>
> First of all, he must pretend he cannot see spears. Even when they are coming straight at him. Secondly, he must also learn to duck very quickly. Lastly, he must pretend nothing at all happened.
>
> You can easily tell when someone has been hit by a spear. He turns a deep shade of bitter. David never got hit. Gradually, he learned a very well kept secret. He discovered three things that prevented him from ever being hit.
>
> One, never learn anything about the fashionable, easily-mastered art of spear throwing.
>
> Two, stay out of the company of all spear throwers.
>
> And three, keep your mouth tightly closed.

In this way, spears will never touch you, even when they pierce your heart.⁵⁶

Strikingly, Edwards's admonishment in this chapter is exactly the espoused theology of senior PAOC leaders on the abuse of ministers: subordinate clergy must endure attack as a form of spiritual faithfulness, they must be continuously unarmed and vulnerable, and in particular they must keep their mouths "tightly closed" concerning the abuse they see and endure. The present task is to evaluate this work as a normative model; is the framework that Edwards has provided suitable for responding to clergy conflict within the context of power differentials?

Critiquing the Espoused Voice

While the dramatized account of David and Saul's interactions is intriguing, it is nonetheless inappropriate for use as a prescriptive model. Developing a normative theology based on an analogous reading of David's experiences in 1 Sam 19:8–10 poses a significant risk for the reader. Further, by casting Saul as a potentially normative spiritual leader and frequently citing his credentials as "the Lord's anointed,"⁵⁷ Edwards's potentially legitimizes leadership behaviour that is blatantly condemned in both the Torah (a clear violation of the "Bill of Other People's Rights" by one with power and authority)⁵⁸ and the New Testament, which clearly affirms the anthropological priority of the Sinaitic code before articulating even higher standards for those who lead in the church.⁵⁹ To espouse *A Tale of Three Kings* as normative theology, a template to be used by clergy facing mistreatment, is thus entirely inappropriate,

---

56. Edwards, *Tale of Three Kings*, 22.

57. Within 1 Samuel it is worth noting that while David refers to Saul as "the Lord's anointed," this perspective is never explicitly endorsed by God; further, the account in Edwards's book takes place after Saul is explicitly rejected as Israel's legitimate king (1 Sam 15:26).

58. Imes, *Bearing God's Name*, 53; Exod 20:13.

59. Matt 5:43–45; Col 3:8; 1 Tim 3:1–7.

as is the associated marginalization of clergy who break from this model and stand up to their tyrants.

The level at which Edwards's work resonates within the sample group ought to give rise to a serious pause: there are spear-throwing "Saul's" among PAOC clergy, but rather than identify and discipline them, those in positions of trust have opted to burden their victims with the responsibility of "learning a lesson" from such abuse. While the "spears" documented in this research vary from denigrating comments (in particular, racial or sexist remarks) to outright threats, the consistency with which the victims of such attacks report passivity by senior leadership further demonstrate the widespread acceptance of Edwards's model.[60] Notwithstanding the continued popularity of Edwards's book,[61] its message likewise finds itself at odds with the serious scholarly work of both DeGroat and Mullen (reviewed in the previous chapter).

Beyond the potential of both legal consequence and further impacts to long-term sustainability, Diane Langberg articulates the spiritual cost of continuing along the present course:

> [In speaking out about abuse], the youth pastor "disobeyed" those God had put over him . . . voices were silenced. Power was abused in order to accomplish that. . . . To treat any human, a person created in God's image, as less than human is destructive to their personhood, their identity. The God who called the Word intends for those create in his image to have a voice. He created us to speak. He does not want that voice silenced or crushed.[62]

In absence of support from both the formal and normative theological voices, one must ask, what led to the uncritical adoption of such an unqualified resource? As this model for the

---

60. As noted, in multiple accounts passivity is combined with an appeal to participate in a cover-up scheme for the sake of reputation management, an act aligned with Edwards's prescription that quite literally adds insult to injury.

61. *Tale of Three Kings* maintained a 4.28 out of 5 stars in Good Reads' Community Reviews section as of Aug. 2023 (https://www.goodreads.com/book/show/221282.A_Tale_of_three_Kings#CommunityReviews).

62. Langberg, *Redeeming Power*, 136.

management of power abuse is clearly inadequate, the development of a responsive praxis is urgent. In the aftermath of decades of encouragement for wounded clergy to follow the "steps" within Edwards's book (dodge and run, don't strike back,[63] and above all, stay silent), both clergy and laity would do well to remember that those who throw spears are not shepherds but hunters.

THE RENEWED PRAXIS

Praxis, "the ways in which beliefs and values are enacted and embodied,"[64] is renewed through a process of intentional reflection that roots itself as equally in the ordinary world of decisions, constraints, and unpredictability as it does in the theories, data, and theology of the academy. Returning to the language of the four voices, a renewed praxis emerges when the authoritative voice of normative theology effectively transforms the active voice of operant theology. Of course, this is not a linear act that can simply be mapped out but rather a process that involves a dialogue between all of the voices: the normative is both accessed and obstructed by the established voices of formal and espoused theology within a community, including their critique (or embrace) of the operant voice, as it is, in the present.[65] The "real world" of the operant plays a crucial role in this process, grounding reflection and imagination in practice, while also offering itself up to the other voices for transformation. Of course, values embodied must also be articulated, so as a renewed praxis emerges, a transformation of regular ecclesial language (the espoused voice) should also result. Here, the aim is to engage praxis as a "reflective engagement in history

---

63. A particular disdain for outside intervention is widely noted in the sample. On more than one occasion, district superintendents are reported to have told credentialed clergy that if they took legal action they would "never pastor in the PAOC again"; an overt threat of marginalization.

64 Cartledge, *Practical Theology*, 118.

65. The interaction between the voices engages a kind of epistemological spiral, drawing closer and closer to a faithful articulation of the normative through each pass of reflection and critique.

that transforms the world,"[66] a pushback on the kind of operant theology that is formed haphazardly as a reaction to circumstance.

The current praxis at work in the PAOC is best described as a form of unreflective pragmatism: action, reactions, and entire systems oriented toward the most expedient achievement of a practical end. By virtue of both its history and unique distinctives, the Pentecostal movement has generally held the mission of evangelism and the experience of revival to be the "ends" upon which efforts are focused.[67] Yet in the absence of serious and sustained anthropological reflection, the pursuit of this end has wrought significant collateral damage.[68] While the priorities of gospel proclamation and transformation by the Holy Spirit are faithfully rooted in an appropriate respect for the New Testament narrative, the means of their pursuit varies. Over time, the resources deemed most efficient (and indeed, essential) to the mission have been informally sacralised, making their preservation a primal priority. The assets (such as buildings, trusts, and currency), reputation (of churches, ministers, and the denomination), methods (such as leadership styles, ministry models, and training systems), structures (governance model, by-laws, formal and informal hierarchies) and values (holiness distinctives, theological emphasis, cultural norms) of the PAOC are perceived with varying degrees of indispensability for the cause. Inevitably, the efficient pursuit of mission has, at times, become so deeply conflated with the preservation of these resources, that in a conflict of ethics where addressing the injustice of power abuse might result in reputational damage (or perhaps caring for a member of the clergy might involve revisiting a contested holiness distinctive), the missional

---

66. Cheryl Bridges Johns, *Pentecostal Formation*, as cited in Cartledge, *Practical Theology*, 46.

67. While this point is well established throughout this study, both Wilkinson and Ambrose, *After the Revival*; and Synan, *Century of the Holy Spirit*, provide ample ground for this claim.

68. Consider the totality of the damage wrought within the experiences catalogued in table 2.1 ("Experiences of Indifference"), table 2.2 ("Experiences of Inequality"), table 2.3 ("Experiences of Indignity"), and table 2.4 ("Experiences of Illegal Behaviour").

Theological Response

resources always come first. Unreflective pragmatism leads to the violation of human beings, in part because efficiency, by definition, takes no consideration of ethics; only cost.[69]

An honest admission of this reality is not only painful, it risks producing an epistemological crisis for its members. As reports of abuse, neglect and misconduct are received, the consideration that these experiences are features (not bugs) of an unhealthy system may cast doubt around the legitimacy of the mission and efforts of the organization on the whole. As Langberg notes, religious communities may thus have any number or reasons to engage in a form of cognitive dissonance regarding institutional shortcomings; the threat associated with the acknowledgment of such sins as have been articulated in this research is the perceived nullification of ministry work that so many have devoted their lives to (and with it, the belief of God's supernatural presence within that work).

I propose that the way forward is not in an indiscriminate invalidation of more than one hundred years of Pentecostal ministry in North America but rather the intentional development of a renewed praxis that empowers effective gospel-centered work because of its clergy ethics, and not in spite of them. Achieving this result involves an epistemological shift: away from unreflective pragmatism and toward theological integration.

In action, this renewed praxis centers on answering the question "In this particular time and place, what might it look like to be faithful to God in my treatment of this person?" Further, when faced with great difficulty, it asks, "As a person (or executive body) with significant power, what does it look like to care for those whom God has entrusted to us in the midst of this crisis?"[70] Of course, the answer must be reflectively rooted in both a better

---

69. When efficiency is prioritized, only ethical standards that impose a loss of efficiency are factored. Thus, it is always more efficient to operate within the law, up until breaking the law carries no consequence.

70. This question might serve as a starting point for pragmatic challenges such as budget shortfalls, leadership conflicts, or disciplinary matters. As every question presumes something of the answer, beginning here (with an anthropocentric Christian ethic) sets a trajectory for actions capable of integrating theologically normative priorities.

model of power and an anthropologically informed Christian ethic.[71] This renewed praxis of Christian leadership is judged faithful by measuring whether the character and demeanour of those in power faithfully reflect that of the God in whose name they serve, using all powers according to the kindness, truthfulness, and goodness demonstrated in Christ.

The prioritizing of care for human beings (who are made in God's image) over the preservation of the institution (which is not made in God's image) does not ignore the fiduciary responsibility associated with institutional governance; rather, it appropriately catalyzes it, aligning embedded processes with normative Christian ethics. For those who claim the name of God, the ethical determination of the right use of power considers humans as fundamentally inviolable, exercising positional power with the wellbeing, dignity and flourishing of others as the highest fiduciary duty. This is what it means to "rightly bear God's name."

---

71. As discussed previously in this chapter, a Christian model of power ought to be an expression of love where power is an entrusted gift with which one might serve others.

5

Conclusion and Recommendations

CHAPTER OVERVIEW

WHILE THE RENEWED PRAXIS described in chapter 4 provides a model for engaging change, the specificities of the research data present an opportunity to prescribe fixed recommended practices that might address some of the basic functional deficiencies underlying the abuse of power. This chapter concludes this study by presenting the recommendations that have emerged from analysis of the data in the light of the relevant literature, as well as the embedded consensus emerging from the research participants own answers to the question "In the light of your experience, what would you like to see change in the PAOC?"[1] The implementation

---

1. While prior caution against legislating practical change in isolation still stands (theologically renewed praxis requires dialogue between the theoretical and the practical), as an extension of the analysis completed in ch. 4 these recommendations are presented as a "first step" to change. They are not all-encompassing. To that end, while policies or procedures on their own cannot change the heart of a leader who has misused power in a significant way, they do provide a slow introduction to transformation. Should those in power find themselves honouring the personhood of their subordinates more fully, even if only due to mandated processes, they are still participating (no matter how small) in the application of normative theological anthropology. Thus, the value of better policies should not be underestimated as they may be the first means by which stubborn leaders experience God's promise to "remove from you your heart of stone and give you a heart of flesh" (Ezek 36:26).

of best practices is an important step in reforming systems where the misuse of power has been demonstrated; as James Poling notes, even small institutional changes are acts of redemptive power.

> Those who are powerful can organize societies in such a way that those who are vulnerable are denied the full resources that life has to offer. Abuse of power relies on institutions and ideologies.[2]

This chapter is organized into three broad sections: recommended practices, the challenge of narcissism, and "an attitude of grace," which seeks to answer the question of how the renewed praxis might be applied to those who find their past behaviour squarely confronted within this work. Finally, a concluding summary is provided as the last word. As chapter 4 has spoken clearly to the ideological considerations of this study, we now turn our attention to the institution.

RECOMMENDED PRACTICES FOR THE PAOC

Despite the diversity of the sample and its experiences, a common set of recommended practices address the vast majority of issues raised. The following recommendations represent minimum steps that, if taken, would have significantly mitigated harm, or provided recourse.

Acknowledgment of Complicity

There is a general sentiment in the sample that the PAOC (as an institution) is unwilling to acknowledge the scope and impact of the harm clergy have experienced as a direct result of the misuse of power. Sadly, the debate over whether abuse of power in the PAOC is an actual problem or merely an exaggerated concern stemming from a small number of individuals continues to surface

---

2. Poling, *Abuse of Power*, 29.

in multiple forums.[3] While recent public initiatives to address and explore the issue of abuse of power are important, there has yet to be a statement which includes any admission of culpability on behalf of the institution.[4] Dave's remarks at the conclusion of his interview are unsurprising. "I feel like the PAOC needs to recognize [this problem] publicly. And apologize. I think there needs to be a public apology."[5]

As the silencing of clergy, after their already having been mistreated, was unequivocally experienced as a second assault, the antipodal response has the potential to be equally powerful in the task of healing and restoration. In much the same way that passivity and indifference can exacerbate the pain of these experiences, acknowledgment is the first step in the reconciliatory process. The emotional and psychological distress that abused clergy have endured has largely been addressed through a significant number of hours with professional therapists, a cost overwhelmingly borne by the victims of the abuse themselves.[6] As a practical acknowledgment of complicity, the District and General Conferences must also develop a fund to offset and reimburse the cost of psychotherapy for current and former clergy whose emotional and spiritual injuries are directly related to systemic passivity.

Continuing Education

Multiple participants (all with senior leadership experience) raised significant questions regarding the absence of mandatory and continuing professional education in the PAOC, particularly when

3. Private source.

4. This is no small matter, considering the prevalence of "Passivity (Systemic)" within the research data.

5. Interview transcript S1P11.

6. Psychotherapy benefits in the PAOC vary but are inadequate to cover extended therapy related to significant experiences of abuse in the workplace. For example, clergy within the EOND with access to Class P1 Group Benefits received a reimbursement to a maximum of $400 per calendar year in 2023. Those who resign their credentials following an experience of abuse are unable to access this care.

coupled with a lack of available college or seminary material on relevant subjects.[7] One lead pastor of a large, multi-staff church specifically noted, "I've never had any HR training or power-differential training [as a lead pastor]. Why isn't continuing education required as part of credential renewal?"[8] Another remarked that they were surprised to have received no resources when they entered a lead pastor role and further acknowledged there was no system of accountability for how they treated their staff.[9] A further demonstration of this training gap surfaces in the occurrence of illegal and inappropriate lines of questioning during employment interviews.[10]

Today, every recognized profession in Canada requires continuing education, including self-regulated industries.[11] This puts the PAOC significantly out of step with Canadian expectations of professionalism for those in positions of trust.[12] A continuing education program that includes training on power and ethics is particularly important for senior leaders:

7. The subjects identified were employment law, acceptable HR practices, professional ethics (including the ethics that surround power differentials), and basic management.

8. Source withheld for confidentiality.

9. Field notes S1P11. Similar comment in interview transcript S1P5.

10. In addition to experiences described by the participants of the study, during the course of this project the researcher was contacted by a student at a PAOC college who had been interviewed for a position by a panel that included a well-known leader with significant national influence; they reported inappropriate questions related to their partner, future plans regarding children, parental leave, and details about private finances. Upon resisting these questions, they were chastised. Such anecdotes appear to be common and may warrant further investigation.

11. Dolik, "Continuing Education Requirements." At the time of writing, each regulatory body, including self-regulatory organizations, require all licensed, certified, or professional members to complete mandatory continuing education. For a complete list of regulated professions in Canada, see OCASI, "Where Can I Get Information."

12. This is especially true when considering that other denominations have implemented continuing education policies. See Anglican Diocese of Ottawa, *Lay Reader Manual*; Presbyterian Church in Canada, "Continuing Education Regulations."

Conclusion and Recommendations

Research on power and compassion/empathy has shown that elevated social power is associated with a diminished reciprocal emotional response to another's sufferings. In other words, the more power a person holds in relation to other people, the less empathy they will have.[13]

At bare minimum, the PAOC must mandate a national continuing education program that offers appropriate certification level training in professional ethics and employment law, correlating to a new by-law standard that would require the completion of such courses prior to appointment to a supervisory role.

Independent HR

The significance of labour-related mistreatment specifically demonstrates the need for accessible HR professionals. As outlined in chapter 2, complaints of employment standard violations are frequent,[14] and the absence of trained HR professionals within most PAOC affiliated entities represents an anachronistic liability on multiple levels.[15] As Jennifer, lamented, "I think that in the Christian world, we never want to think that a pastor [would] harass another pastor, so we don't build a system in case it happens . . . [but] in my case, when it did happen, I was asked to lie to people about why I left."[16] Samantha, commenting specifically on her experiences of sexual harassment, noted, "We can't have

---

13. Langberg, *Redeeming Power*, 132, in reference to Van Kleef et al., "Power, Distress, and Compassion."

14. These include workplace harassment and discrimination, contract violations, constructive dismissal, and post-departure retaliation, in addition to excessive hours and forced volunteerism.

15. The consistent failure of employers to provide subordinate clergy within the sample with even the most basic labour standards afforded to them by Canadian law is well documented. Other HR functions, such as handling complaints of misconduct, are likewise not adequately managed via present means. The sample further included multiple accounts of district officers operating in bad faith or with conflict of interest in the favour of a personal friend. For additional examples of labour complaints, see table 2.2.

16. Interview transcript.

conversations with people that are offside from an HR perspective. I don't think it's good enough to just say, "Oh that? That's just [name withheld] talking to me, [as a young female pastor], about sex. There must be consequences for that kind of thing. And we must clearly state that those kinds of conversations aren't appropriate."[17] Rose noted, "Everyone should have an exit interview, and not by the person you were abused by."[18]

The call for access to an HR department that operates independently from the direct employer was a consistent participant recommendation in response to nearly universal agreement that there is simply no body of advocacy for credential holders who are not lead pastors during any dispute that involves a power differential.[19] Such a department would also provide a safe avenue for "whistleblower" reports, in addition to serving the fellowship by providing confidential exit interview services, thus yielding data that may play a role in strategies to improve overall clergy retention.

It is therefore recommended that certified HR professionals, hired under a shared-service model,[20] be empowered with the authority to investigate complaints, mandate legal and policy compliance, recommend disciplinary action, and hold all credential

---

17. Interview transcript.

18. Interview transcript.

19. Tom noted specifically that there is truth to the perception of district favouritism for lead pastors, and cited a significant (and pleasant) change in his relationship with the district officers after having been appointed a lead pastor. He noted that upon becoming a lead pastor, "I can call anytime . . . they always have my back." Tom noted this was not his experience as a youth pastor. One participant lamented that the DE in his district is "a room full of lead pastors protecting other lead pastors"; a sentiment reflected among other participants. It is especially significant to note that female lead pastors interviewed did not report the same level of perceived support from their district officers, whom they described as indifferent to them at best.

20. The shared-service model is one whereby the expense of operation can be equally divided on a prorated basis to all PAOC entities (for example, based on the number of employees). This ensures both affordability and equity, giving all institutions and credential holders access.

holders accountable (regardless of role or status) while operating at arm's length from both the local churches and the district offices.

Mandated Minimum Compliance

As recently as August 2023, the PAOC sent an internal email to credential holders updating the constituency on action steps related to the working group's recommendation for addressing abuse of power. The email included a video link for "one of several resources to come that would equip pastors, leaders, and ministries by heightening awareness of the rightful use of authority and practical steps to avoid abuses of power."[21] In the video, Tanya Rust, a registered psychotherapist engaged by the PAOC, provides an overview of power dynamics and then recommends that all churches develop a workplace harassment and whistleblower policy that includes the designation of a compliance officer to ensure confidentiality for complainants.

Without discouraging the future development of educational resources, the difficulty with recommended actions such as this is their optionality; considering the number of mandatory requirements readily imposed upon PAOC churches, entities, and credential holders,[22] a special meeting to amend the by-laws in order to require (not recommend) nationalized standard workplace harassment and whistleblower policies must take place.[23] As the General Conference has already amended by-law 10 to include "abuse of power," this recommendation presents an opportunity to codify the supportive framework required to fully address the

---

21. Private source.

22. Notwithstanding by-law 3.3, which states that "this local church shall have the right to develop policies and procedures which guide its operation," it must be noted that to become an affiliated church several policies and procedures are mandatory, including financial requirements (by-law 2.1) and complying with provincial nonprofit or registered societies legislation and the Federal Tax Act (by-laws 2.4, 2.6).

23. Noting that some of these policies may already be legally required in certain provinces, a national standard would provide all clergy the same level of protection, regardless of their district.

issue. This form of self-regulation is especially needed in light of the unique structure of the PAOC.[24]

Second, as abuse of power is not limited to local church contexts, the video resource did not fully address strategies of mitigation for power abuse perpetuated by district or national personnel. Legislating best practices improves all workplaces (whether local, district, or national) by limiting the influence of favouritism, establishing clear recourse for those who experience discrimination, and providing a layer of protection for retaliatory action.

---

24. Because the General Constitution is administrated by the general executive, credentials are administered by each district executive, and employment is administered at the local level, there are multiple loopholes by which employees can be disenfranchised or where they are not protected by law. For example, a member of the clergy can be dismissed at the local level as a result of having their credentials revoked by their district (for any number of reasons related to by-law 10 in the General Constitution, which is administered by the general executive, or at a national level). While this structure has been internally noted as essential in order to protect churches from human rights litigation if the termination of a pastor who departs from the PAOC's statement of faith is required, this structure may also be used to protect all parties from litigation over a bona fide wrongful termination; inversely, it protects the general executive (who is not a direct employer) from accountability over various points in the General Constitution that may otherwise be unacceptable under Canadian employment law.

A specific example of the abuse of this structure was reported within the sample group: a pastor was discriminated against by a credential holder with significant power and influence based on characteristics protected by the human rights code. When the pastor sought to address this issue, they were first exhorted to "let it go" by their district superintendent. Refusing, the pastor was then alleged to be "uncooperative" with district leadership, with full awareness that such a charge could constitute a disciplinary hearing that might result in removal of credentials, leading the pastor to then be terminated by their direct employer, who would be shielded from liability (they are merely terminating a pastor who no longer holds credentials). A lack of confidence in the impartiality of a disciplinary panel, should the charge have been filed, weighed heavily on the discriminated pastor. In this case, the organizational structure of the PAOC was weaponized in order to limit the option of recourse for a pastor, simultaneously denying their charter rights as a Canadian.

Prohibition of NDAs

As noted in chapter 2, there does not appear to be a single legitimate ethical use for NDAs within the ecclesial context.[25] Despite this, there are multiple references to NDAs within the sample; in each case, they were used to protect the institution or a powerful leader from accountability for misconduct. In this light, it is recommended that a resolution be brought before the General Conference of the PAOC to universally prohibit the use of NDAs within the denomination, a course of action already overdue.[26]

Theological Renewal

As noted throughout this study, the minimization of theological anthropology in the formal doctrinal expressions of the PAOC is echoed in espoused voices of the movement. Notwithstanding the breadth of Christian theology and the need for a concise statement of faith, a formal commission of trained Pentecostal theologians to the production of a new position paper on power, anthropology, and ethics (with accompanying recommendation of amendment to the SOET) is required. While operant practices may be initially reformed by policies and mandates, for the PAOC to develop a truly renewed operant theology, formal work must be done and then reflected into the espoused voice of the movement.

---

25. See "The Role of NDAs" in ch. 2.

26. As previously noted, the 2023 decision by the Canadian Bar Association to prohibit the use of NDAs for silencing complaints of harassment, abuse and discrimination only furthers this point (Bhat and Schmunk, "Lawyers Across Canada," paras. 1–2, 14–15).

Power in Practice

THE CHALLENGE OF NARCISSISM[27]

Identifying the Threat

As noted in the literature, the threat that narcissism presents to religious institutions must not be underestimated. The American Psychological Association lists nine traits associated with pathological narcissism:

1. A grandiose sense of self-importance.
2. A preoccupation with success, power, or brilliance.
3. A belief that they are "special" and elite.
4. An expectation of excessive admiration.
5. A false sense of entitlement (expecting favorable treatment).
6. A willingness to take advantage of others for their own ends.
7. A lack empathy for others.

---

27. Clinically speaking, narcissism is a set of pathological traits outlined in the list of DSM-V TR Cluster B Personality Disorders (American Psychiatric Association, *DSM-5-TR*, 761–62). DeGroat notes that this clinical narcissism exists on a scale from "healthy" (confident but humble; considerate of others) to "toxic" (exploitive, entitled, selfish) or even "malignant" (manipulative, callously indifferent, cruel); further, healthy and toxic traits can be expressed as styles, types, and diagnosable pathologies (DeGroat, *When Narcissism Comes to Church*, 35–37, 41, 51–52). As a result, he cautions the reader from casually applying clinical labels to others, as only clinicians with the proper tools and training should make such diagnosis. See DeGroat, *When Narcissism Comes to Church*, 36, fig. 2.1.

Notwithstanding this cautionary note, DeGroat is equally adamant that toxic and malignant forms of narcissism present an acute risk to the life and health of the church, a concern supported by the research data collected in this study. It is in this light that the topic of narcissism will be cautiously engaged, with usage of the terms *narcissism* and *narcissist* reflecting DeGroat's own usage throughout his book as a general shorthand for the observable characteristics associated with toxic and malignant behaviours, sometimes called "trait narcissism." References to "narcissistic pastors" within this section should be understood merely as a reference to pastors who are perceived to be exhibiting the traits associated to DeGroat's descriptions of the same, and not necessarily pastors who have been specifically diagnosed with NPD (narcissistic personality disorder) by a clinician.

Conclusion and Recommendations

8. An envious (or inappropriately competitive) outlook.
9. An arrogant or haughty attitude and behaviour.[28]

Within these traits lies a particular capacity to exploit the ecclesial system due to assumptions of shared values. A community that presumes the love of neighbor as normative has an especially limited capacity to conceive of leaders who might pursue their own self-interest, regardless of the cost to others. The embedded ethics of the Christian faith, not least of which includes an expectation of truthfulness and integrity, are ill prepared to respond such willingness to subvert boundaries and policies through lies and manipulation. Further, the narcissist's core need to reinforce their distorted self-image makes Christian leadership attractive.

> A colleague of mine often says that ministry is a magnet for a narcissistic personality—who else would want to speak on behalf of God every week? While the vast majority of people struggle with public speaking, not only do pastors do it regularly, but they do it with "divine authority."[29]

Within the sample, there is evidence that several participants encountered leaders with traits similar to those described in literature on narcissism. The sample produced multiple overlapping accounts of serial offenders who "spin" the facts into various forms of untruth in order to further their personal agenda and escape accountability,[30] a striking observation considering that, typologically, the narcissistic pastor is the ultimate "bullshitter."[31]

---

28. American Psychiatric Association, "What Is Narcissistic Personality Disorder?"

29. DeGroat, *When Narcissism Comes to Church*, 19.

30. In addition to the primary offence, Blodgett would argue that these acts of "bullshitting" represent an important secondary point of moral injury to those affected.

31. As cited in ch. 3, Blodgett defines *bullshit* as the "false statements that are not necessarily factually untrue but nevertheless have the effect of steering the hearer away from the truth. There are things people say without the conscious intention of deceiving others but with so little concern for veracity that the truth often ends up being misrepresented anyway. . . . Defined in

Clear examples of other narcissistic behavioural patterns, such as described by Mullen, are also documented repeatedly: for example, the "dismantling" of Wayne's sense of self through "intimidation, humiliation, and outright violence to produce feelings of fear and shame,"[32] an experience shared by Joseph, Mila, Diane, Hans, and Rose.[33] There is an urgent need for an informed strategic response.[34]

Responding to Narcissism in Clergy

In Canada, the subject of psychological screening is a sensitive topic. Rightly, the Human Rights Code protects prospective employees from discrimination on any protected ground, including medical conditions and disabilities.[35] Notwithstanding, there

---

contrast to liars, bullshitters do not care one way or the other about the truth and deceive their listeners by pretending to be sincere and authentic" (*Lives Entrusted*, 136, 3.)

32. Mullen, *Something's Not Right*, 53. Experiences in table 2.3 are especially indicative of narcissistic-type traits.

33. A comprehensive comparison to Mullen, DeGroat and Langberg's material of the specific accounts of the participants, including the experiences summarized in ch. 2, is alarming. The characteristics of the tactics employed by those alleged to have engaged in misconduct bears significant correlation to the literature.

34. DeGroat notes that denominations with nontraditional ordination processes that do not require a Master of Divinity at an associated seminary or where "young leaders are snatched up and deployed without proper training or soul formation, simply because they've been successful in other arenas," are far more likely to see narcissistic exploitation (*When Narcissism Comes to Church*, 21).

The vulnerability of young clergy is exacerbated by their lack of maturity and education (especially those who do not finish their prescribed program before beginning ministry) in addition to the personal sense of indebtedness they experience toward those who have recruited them. In light of the observed interest at the 2022 PAOC General Conference to provide simpler pathways for "called" young people to enter pastoral roles (prior to the completion of even a three-year ministerial diploma) and the arguments made in favour of restructuring Master's College & Seminary to prioritize "hub churches" for local church-based training in 2024, DeGroat's caution is even more significant.

35. See Ontario Human Rights Commission, *Minds That Matter*; Essential

CONCLUSION AND RECOMMENDATIONS

are multiple Canadian institutions that engage in significant psychological suitability screening as part of their hiring processes, though generally this is limited to professions where security clearance is required.[36] This selectivity reflects the legal standard applied to determine whether any form of preemployment screening is permissible, namely, can it be demonstrated that the screening is directly related to a bona fide requirement for safe and satisfactory completion of the duties of the job?[37] While the particular traits of NPD are well associated with levels of unacceptable risk for those employed in positions related to national security,[38] it may be far more difficult to reasonably demonstrate that these risks justify psychological screening of potential clergy.[39]

The vulnerability of a person participating in psychological screening is significant; the process creates an enormous power differential with those who have mandated the process, and there's a significant capacity for misuse of both the system and the data generated. Thus, the Canadian regulatory framework, which carefully sets limits on how such tools can be used in relation to employment, is reasonable.[40] In balancing the need to protect the privacy and dignity of individuals with the fiduciary responsibility to mitigate a clear risk to the well-being of the wider religious

---

HR, "Personality Tests When Hiring"; Seward, *Balancing Workplace Mental Health Issues*.

36. Examples being various departments of the federal government, where information related to national security is at stake, and in the policing sector, where the use of deadly force is foreseeable (Government of Canada, "Public Service Commission Approval"; Royal Canadian Mounted Police, "Become a Police Officer," s.vv. "6. Undergo Medical and Psychological Assessments").

37. Essential HR, "Personality Tests When Hiring."

38. See Shechter and Lang, *Identifying Personality Disorders*, 2–5; Beshears, "Why Narcissism Cannot Be Ignored."

39. Despite both a strong case that religious environments are exceptionally vulnerable to manipulation and DeGroat's own professional experience in administering such screening within the United States (DeGroat, *When Narcissism Comes to Church*, 19), there is simply no use case in Canada that would present the assumption this course of action would be appropriate.

40. Particularly in light of the discussion on models of power and the priority of anthropocentric ethics in ch. 4.

community, an application of the renewed praxis, articulated in chapter 4, is appropriate.

Engaging this model, the question can be asked, "How might the PAOC love and serve clergy candidates through the process of risk mitigation?" From this perspective, the development of a confidential, collaborative, and genuinely altruistic framework of comprehensive psychological support, focused on clergy self-awareness and mental health, is ideal. Rather than merely seeking to identify narcissistic traits,[41] the integration of a regulated and confidential psychological health component into the PAOC credential application process presents an opportunity to proactively invest in the long-term health of all clergy.[42] Perhaps most significantly, this provides an opportunity to mitigate the impact of narcissism via an indirect approach: candidates who exhibit elevated narcissistic traits might be presented with an early and confidential opportunity to address the significant burdens of shame, insecurity, and anxiety that often predispose and exacerbate traits related to NPD.[43] Meanwhile, others who demonstrate greater emotional vulnerability to the manipulative tactics of toxic and malignant narcissists might also be proactively educated and supported, in order to reduce their risk of exploitation. While it is conceivable that a small number of individuals with more significant narcissistic traits may simply refuse to engage in transformative work (or even refuse to participate in a system with a proactive process),[44]

---

41. As expressions of narcissism exist on a scale, the mere presence of an elevated NPD score on an assessment ought not to automatically disqualify someone from pastoral work. As DeGroat makes note, those who are self-aware enough to engage in healthy relationships, typically referred to as "healthy narcissists," do have the capacity to make excellent ministers (*When Narcissism Comes to Church*, 32).

42. Proactive programs such as this are both common and legally sound, and are engaged in the selection, hiring, and ongoing support of multiple professionals, including first responders and those in high-stress business professions (Seward, *Balancing Workplace Mental Health Issues*).

43. DeGroat, *When Narcissism Comes to Church*, 19.

44. As DeGroat notes, "Antisocial personality disorder (APD), sometimes called sociopathy, is deeply alarming and painful when it shows up in ecclesial and ministry settings. Indeed, though the DSM-V has not yet recognized it

the benefit of helping those who are willing to engage psychological help cannot be understated. Coupled with a proactive continuing education program to ensure that the "tactics" of narcissists are exposed and disavowed,[45] the risk of narcissistic manipulation in the PAOC might be greatly reduced.

In regard to current ministers (those already credentialed and serving within the denomination), voluntary access to the same clergy health initiative should be provided. While mandating retroactive participation would be inappropriate, in the case that a credential holder is found guilty of abuse of power (in accordance with by-law 10), it is not unreasonable that psychological intervention would be mandated as a responsive measure to determine the nature of the restoration program most appropriate. Considering the high likelihood that diagnosably narcissistic pastors will abuse power, proceeding to offer restoration to the minister while remaining uninformed by an appropriately administered psychological assessment would be irresponsible.

While the scope and cost of such an initiative may appear daunting, this systematic approach to compassionate and proactive care within the PAOC affords an opportunity for the significant benefits that accompany a wide network of emotionally healthy clergy.

Responding to Narcissism in the Institution

While narcissistic traits are most commonly ascribed to individuals, DeGroat notes that impersonal systems, or institutional cultures, can themselves take on the characteristics associated with

---

as an official, clinical category, some theorists have chosen the term 'malignant narcissism' to describe the narcissist with sociopathic behaviors. Prone to callous indifference, manipulation, and rule breaking, APD shows up often among pastoral predators who use and abuse their power to exploit others" (*When Narcissism Comes to Church*, 41). He further notes that those afflicted this way are most likely to select relationships and employment opportunities that demonstrate low resistance to their tendencies.

45. For an overview of tactics, see the list provided in ch. 3, included in the section titled "Mullen: Something's Not Right."

NPD, influencing leaders to ignore the damage to human beings inflicted by callous policies and priorities.

> Narcissistic systems exist for themselves, even though their mission statements and theological beliefs may be filled with the language of service, selflessness, justice, and care. . . . Disconnected from the reality of the system's dysfunction or narcissistic sepsis, the members collude in a collective act of glancing lovingly into the pool of water that reflects back the ideal image, just as a narcissistic pastor might.[46]

DeGroat, Mullen, and Langberg further note that depersonalized systems that have internalized narcissistic traits can be even more damaging to individuals than a single narcissist abusing power.[47]

The incongruence between the espoused voice of the PAOC (documented as district and national leaders frequently speaking to the care and concern for all clergy) and the operant voice (as noted, the demonstration of indifference and the wide proliferation of retaliation to those who report mistreatment) was lamented by participants in this study.[48] Such a gap is indicative of a false institutional self-perception, a core narcissistic trait. Accordingly, the appropriate response is reflective of the approach to the effective

---

46. DeGroat, *When Narcissism Comes to Church*, 24, 104.

47. Langberg's foreword in Mullen's *Something's Not Right* (xvi), references the same concerns that she names in her own book, namely that "the abuse of a Christian system multiplies exponentially the damage done by a single perpetrator," (Langberg, *Redeeming Power*, 147). Further, Mullen is careful to note the role that systems play in the harm of individuals (*Something's Not Right*, 24–28). DeGroat's concerns are likewise well documented with two case studies (*When Narcissism Comes to Church*, 104–10).

48. It is significant that the research participants provided a composite description of the institutional character of the PAOC using the same terms DeGroat applies to narcissists: unapologetic, indifferent, and capable of both passive and active malevolence when confronted (DeGroat, *When Narcissism Comes to Church*, 41). Beyond the individual case studies presented in ch. 2, these descriptions were present in a significant form in each interview as a response to the question "How did your experiences impact your relationship with the PAOC?"

intervention of an individual: gracious but unflinching honesty, or "speaking the truth in love" (Eph 4:15). Objective assessments, along with open dialogue and a refusal to "bullshit," are essential.

Committing to an Anthropocentric Christian Ethic

The commitment to realign, whether individually or institutionally, with anthropocentric Christian ethics provides the antithesis of narcissism: a commitment to a cruciform model of power, expressed in love. While previously discussed in chapter 4, it bears repeating that the expedient exercise of power to "proclaim the 'Good News' and establish new churches,"[49] can no longer be used to excuse collateral damage in the process. While narcissistic pastors and systems might exhibit a seemingly excellent efficiency in the "success" of these initiatives, the exposure of such achievements as hollow and short term within other denominations and organizations serves as a cautionary tale regarding the cost of narcissistic self-deception within the church.[50]

AN ATTITUDE OF GRACE

While section 2 articulates recommendations related to the care for and protection of victims of power abuse, attention must also be given to those who have perpetrated the acts. The injuries, direct and vicarious, to those who have experienced or witnessed acts of indifference, inequality, and indignity may predispose those impacted to a reactionary posture. It is, perhaps, only natural to desire punitive accountability for perceived perpetrators.

There is therefore a practical need to formulate a response to the abuse of power that reflects Christ's command to love one's enemy and bless one's persecutors (Matt 5:43–44; Rom 12:14),

---

49. Wells, "Aligned for Mission," para. 7.
50. See Sasha, "Secrets of Hillsong"; Taylor, "Carl Lentz"; Jones, "Hillsong's High and Low Notes"; Cosper, "Who Killed Mars Hill?"; Roys, "James MacDonald Is Fired."

without further enabling abuse nor ignoring the betrayal associated with mistreatment from those operating in the name of Christ.[51] While the case has been made that ignoring abuse of power is antithetical to Christian ethics, it must also be noted that graciousness for the sinner stands at the epicentre of the same.

The fear of exposure and punishment works against the formation of any healthy system by driving those guilty of offences to hide their misdeeds while continuing to live from the personal dysfunction that led to such transgressions in the first place.[52] Further, in the contemporary era, the phenomenon of "cancel culture" (where certain mistakes demand eternal shaming, with no possibility of redemption),[53] subtly offers its services to Christians as a means for addressing misdeeds. While contributing factors in the formation of abusive tendencies do not absolve a leader of responsibility for their mistreatment of others, they do demonstrate the complexities of the present situation and call for a response toward the perpetrator of abuse that is as equally aligned with the Christian ethos as the other recommendations in this project endeavour to be.[54]

In order to fully address the systemic risk of power abuse, the fear of exposure must be offset through the provision of an off-ramp from dysfunction: an opportunity for healing and restoration for those who voluntarily recognize their culpability in the gross mistreatment of others. Certainly, as DeGroat notes, "some will resist, and the walls of the hell they've chosen will crush them,"[55] yet the promise that "there will be more rejoicing in heaven over

---

51. In essence, there is a need to provide an alternative to Albert Poirier's efforts of the same nature (*Peacemaking Pastor*).

52. Langberg, *Redeeming Power*, 35.

53. Dudenhoefer, "Is Cancel Culture Effective?"

54. Considering the role that shame pays in the formation of narcissistic behaviour, and the chronological cross section of the experiences reported in the research (it should be noted that participants related consistent accounts of abuse of power extending back to at least the 1980s), the likelihood that the even the most prolific perpetrators of abuse of power in the PAOC are also victims of the same is quite significant.

55. DeGroat, *When Narcissism Comes to Church*, 163.

one sinner who repents than over ninety-nine righteous persons who do not need to repent" (Luke 15:7) must be embraced. Reflecting on the theological anthropology that underpins this study, one cannot fail to recognize that those who have wounded others are nonetheless image bearers themselves; thus, failing to offer the certainty of love and dignity alongside a process of remediation and restitution would be a deep hypocrisy.

As Imes emphasizes, alongside the priority of Israel to "bear the name of the Lord" in righteous faithfulness there is a stunning juxtaposition:

> The Israelites had agreed to the terms of the covenant, but God's first order of business was articulating to Moses the means by which they could be forgiven for breaking that covenant.[56]

A Christian response to sin must reflect this ethos, even as corrective and restorative processes are developed. Shame, that insidious tool of evil, is no more fit for the work of remediation than it is be used as a tool of abuse in the first place. In this light, initiatives to prevent further abuse of power (such as clergy care and continuing education) must remain continuously rooted in an understanding of Christian vocation as a call to care for one another, lest they devolve into strategies to motivate by fear. The task of carefully creating space for the PAOC's ecclesial community to bear witness to the suffering of the mistreated, while simultaneously refusing to foster hatred and "cancellation" of those who have sinned, is a difficult task achievable only by the grace of God and the power of the Holy Spirit; perhaps a task especially appropriate for the Pentecostal church, which holds steadfast to the belief such empowerment is available. To this end, a gracious but serious dialogue must take place.

---

56. Imes, *Bearing God's Name*, 67.

RESEARCH CONCLUSION

The purpose of this study has been to examine the experiences of power differentials among PAOC clergy and understand their significance. Locating this study within the discipline of practical theology provided opportunity for theological reflection that addresses the unique context of the PAOC, while also considering the interdisciplinary sources necessary for an informed analysis. As an indicative study, this project makes no formal presumptions regarding the specific quantitative frequency of the participant experiences catalogued within the general body of clergy but concludes, based on the findings, that attention to the scope and specificity of these experiences (including a future quantitative inquiry) by qualified researchers is in order.

The conclusion of this study is that specific experiences of power abuse are common among PAOC clergy, and that the existing structures for safeguarding and remediating these behaviours are inadequate. Further, there is an indication that the leadership body of the denomination is functionally unaware of the gaps between the normative, formal, espoused and operant voices of theology within the movement. In order to arrive at a healthier expression of normative theology (and the resulting ethics), there is a need to foster the development of an ongoing reflective model that might continue to consider the subjects of power, authority, human dignity, and ethics. As the practical recommendations in this chapter are not static, monolithic prescriptions but rather first steps in a process of dynamic transformation, the researcher acknowledges that a theologically informed transformation of practices, metrics, and internal culture will be the result only of an intentional reframing of power as the means to love one another faithfully.

Bibliography

Achkar Law. "Breach of Confidence." Achkar Law, n.d. https://achkarlaw.com/how-to-defend-a-breach-of-confidence-claim/.
Alberta and NWT District. *Church Administration Manual*. PAOC, last updated Dec. 2016. https://paoc.org/docs/default-source/church-toolbox/church-administration/customizable-church-administration-manual/customizable-church-administration-manual.docx?sfvrsn=1374e06a_2.
———. *Church Leadership Philosophy Manual for [Name of Church]*. PAOC, Jan. 2016. https://paoc.org/docs/default-source/church-toolbox/church-administration/customizable-church-administration-manual/tabs-details/tab-l/church-leadership-philosophy-manual.doc?sfvrsn=877ce06a_2.
Ambrose, Linda M., and Martin W. Mittelstaedt. "Belief and Practice: Canadian Pentecostal Case Studies." *Canadian Journal of Pentecostal-Charismatic Christianity* 9 (2018) i–iii.
American Psychiatric Association. *Diagnostic and Statistical Manual of Mental Disorders: DSM-5-TR*. 5th ed. Washington, DC: American Psychiatric Association, 2022.
———. "What Is Narcissistic Personality Disorder?" Psychiatry, Jan. 30, 2024. https://www.psychiatry.org/news-room/apa-blogs/what-is-narcissistic-personality-disorder.
Anglican Diocese of Ottawa. *Lay Reader Manual: Learning to Serve*. Diocese of Ottawa, 2021. https://ottawa.anglican.ca/wp-content/uploads/2023/12/Lay-Reader-Manual-2021-Revised-May-4-2021.pdf.
Bailey, Jon Nelson. "Vowing Away the Fifth Commandment: Matthew 15:3–6 // Mark 7:9–13." *Restoration Quarterly* 42 (2000) 193–209.
Beale, G. K., and D. A. Carson, ed. *Commentary on the New Testament Use of the Old Testament*. 4th ed. Grand Rapids: Baker Academic, 2009.
Beasley-Murray, Paul. *Power for God's Sake: Power and Abuse in the Local Church*. Carlisle, UK: Paternoster, 1998.
Beaty, Katelyn. *Celebrities for Jesus: How Personas, Platforms, and Profits Are Hurting the Church*. Grand Rapids: Brazos, 2022.

Bibliography

Bedard, Robert. "Emerging Models of Ministerial Training for Pentecostal Assemblies of Canada." DTh diss., University of South Africa, 2008. https://uir.unisa.ac.za/server/api/core/bitstreams/20ad2834-2ebf-40f0-ae7a-91328478bb9c/content.

Beshears, Michael. "Why Narcissism Cannot Be Ignored by Public Safety Leadership." Gov1, Dec. 26, 2019. https://www.gov1.com/public-safety/articles/why-narcissism-cannot-be-ignored-by-public-safety-leadership-Vv4GNzrWokYGudAd/.

Bhat, Priyana, and Rhianna Schmunk. "Lawyers Across Canada Approve Groundbreaking Resolution to Help Prevent Abuse of Non-Disclosure Agreements." CBC, Feb. 9, 2023. https://www.cbc.ca/news/canada/british-columbia/lawyers-across-canada-approve-groundbreaking-resolution-to-help-prevent-abuse-of-non-disclosure-agreements-1.6741976.

Biggs, Reinette, et al., eds. *The Routledge Handbook of Research Methods for Social-Ecological Systems*. Routledge Environment and Sustainability Handbooks. New York: Routledge, 2021.

Blodgett, Barbara J. *Lives Entrusted: An Ethic of Trust for Ministry*. Prisms. Minneapolis: Fortress, 2008.

Boecker, Hans Jochen. *Law and the Administration of Justice in the Old Testament and Ancient East*. Minneapolis: Augsburg, 1980.

Bosman, Jasper. "Celebrating the Lord's Supper in the Netherlands: A Study of Liturgical Ritual Practice in Dutch Reformed Churches." *Yearbook for Ritual and Liturgical Studies* 36 (2020) 146–54.

Brooks, Tiffany Yecke. *Holy Ghosted: Spiritual Anxiety, Religious Trauma and the Language of Abuse*. Grand Rapids: Eerdmans, 2024.

Bruce, F. F. *The Epistle to the Hebrews*. Rev. ed. NICNT. Grand Rapids: Eerdmans, 2009.

Brueggemann, Walter. "The God Who Gives Rest." In *The Book of Exodus: Composition, Reception, and Interpretation*, edited by Thomas B. Dozeman et al., 565–90. VTSup 164. Leiden: Brill, 2014.

Burgess, John P. "A Contemporary Pastoral Rule." In *A Pastoral Rule for Today: Reviving an Ancient Practice*, 163–80. Downers Grove, IL: IVP Academic, 2019.

———. "The Holiness That Stoops to Serve." In *A Pastoral Rule for Today: Reviving an Ancient Practice*, 58–79. Downers Grove, IL: IVP Academic, 2019.

Byrd, Aimee. *The Hope in Our Scars: Finding the Bride of Christ in the Underground of Disillusionment*. Grand Rapids: Zondervan, 2024.

Cameron, Helen, et al. *Talking About God in Practice: Theological Action Research and Practical Theology*. London: SCM, 2010.

Canadian Baptists of Ontario and Quebec. *The Manual of Accreditation and Ordination: Policies and Procedures*. Canadian Baptists of Ontario and Quebec, 2023. https://baptist.ca/wp-content/uploads/2023/01/Accreditation-Manual-March-2023-updated.pdf.

Bibliography

Canadian Jewish News. "Labour Ministry Rules Mashgichim Employees." *Canadian Jewish News*, Dec. 23, 2011. https://thecjn.ca/news/labour-ministry-rules-mashgichim-employees/.

Cartledge, Mark J. *Practical Theology: Charismatic and Empirical Perspectives*. Eugene, OR: Wipf & Stock, 2012.

Churchill, John, et al. "Membership in Secret Orders." PAOC, May 2006. Position Paper. https://paoc.org/docs/default-source/church-toolbox/position-papers/secret-orders/secret-orders.pdf?sfvrsn=266e196a_2.

Corbin, Juliet, and Anselm Strauss. "Grounded Theory Research: Procedures, Canons, and Evaluative Criteria." *Qualitative Sociology* 13 (1990) 3–21. https://doi.org/10.1007/BF00988593.

Cosper, Mike. "The Things We Do to Women." *Christianity Today*, July 6, 2021. https://www.christianitytoday.com/ct/podcasts/rise-and-fall-of-mars-hill/mars-hill-mark-driscoll-podcast-things-we-do-women.html.

———. "Who Killed Mars Hill?" Christianity Today, June 21, 2021. https://www.christianitytoday.com/ct/podcasts/rise-and-fall-of-mars-hill/who-killed-mars-hill-church-mark-driscoll-rise-fall.html.

Creswell, John W., and Cheryl N. Poth. *Qualitative Inquiry & Research Design: Choosing Among Five Approaches*. 4th ed. Los Angeles: SAGE, 2018.

Davis, Ron. "Valuing the Past, Anticipating the Future: Introducing General Secretary Treasurer Craig Burton." *Testimony/Enrich*, Dec. 2022. https://testimony.paoc.org/articles/valuing-the-past-anticipating-the-future.

DeGroat, Chuck. *When Narcissism Comes to Church: Healing Your Community from Emotional and Spiritual Abuse*. Downers Grove, IL: InterVarsity, 2020.

Doctrine Commission of the Church of England. *Being Human: A Christian Understanding of Personhood Illustrated with Reference to Power, Money, Sex and Time*. General Synod 1494. London: Church, 2003.

Dolik, Helen. "Continuing Education Requirements Are Common." *Professionally Speaking: The Publication of the Ontario College of Teachers*, June 2002. https://professionallyspeaking.oct.ca/june_2002/selfreg.asp.

Dudenhoefer, Nicole. "Is Cancel Culture Effective?" *Pegasus: The Magazine of the University of Central Florida*, Fall 2020. https://www.ucf.edu/pegasus/is-cancel-culture-effective/.

Dunlop, Andrew. "Using the 'Four Voices of Theology' in Group Theological Reflection." *Practical Theology* 14 (2021) 294–308.

Edwards, Gene. *A Tale of Three Kings: A Study in Brokenness*. Wheaton, IL: Tyndale, 1992.

Erlacher, Jolene, and Katy White. *Mobilizing Gen Z: Challenges and Opportunities for the Global Age of Missions*. Littleton, CO: William Carey, 2022.

Essential HR. "Personality Tests When Hiring: Proceed With Caution." Essential HR, n.d. https://www.essentialhr.ca/blog/title/personality-tests-when-hiring-proceed-with-caution/id/62/.

Fitch, David E. *Reckoning with Power: Why the Church Fails When It's on the Wrong Side of Power*. Grand Rapids: Brazos 2024.

BIBLIOGRAPHY

Forbes, Cheryl. *The Religion of Power*. London: MARC Europe, 1986.
General Synod of the Anglican Church of Canada. *Competencies for Ordination into the Anglican Church of Canada*. Anglican Church of Canada, 2013. https://www.anglican.ca/wp-content/uploads/2012/04/Competencies_web.pdf.
Giles of Rome. *On Ecclesiastical Power: The "De Ecclesiastica Potestate" of Aegidius Romanus*. Edited and translated by R. W. Dyson. Woodbridge: Boydell, 1986.
Government of Canada. "Copyright Act (R.S.C., 1985, c. C-42)." Justice Laws, 1985. https://laws-lois.justice.gc.ca/eng/acts/c-42/index.html/.
———. "Criminal Code (R.S.C., 1985, c. C-46)." Justice Laws, 1985. https://laws-lois.justice.gc.ca/eng/acts/c-46/FullText.html.
———. "Employment Insurance Act (S.C. 1996, c. 23)." Justice Laws, 1996. https://laws-lois.justice.gc.ca/eng/acts/e-5.6/FullText.html.
———. "Public Service Commission Approval of Psychological Tests." Personnel Psychology Centre, last modified Jan. 15, 2019. https://www.canada.ca/en/public-service-commission/services/staffing-assessment-tools-resources/human-resources-specialists-hiring-managers/human-resources-toolbox/personnel-psychology-centre/consultation-test-services/approval-of-psychological-tests.html.
Greer, Jonathan S., et al., eds. *Behind the Scenes of the Old Testament: Cultural, Social, and Historical Contexts*. Grand Rapids: Baker Academic, 2018.
Greggs, Tom. "Ecclesial Priestly Mediation in the Theology of Dietrich Bonhoeffer." *Theology Today* 71 (2014) 81–91.
Gregory the Great. *Pastoral Rule*. New Advent, n.d. Translated by James Barmby. From $NPNF^2$, edited by Philip Schaff and Henry Wace, vol. 12 (Buffalo, NY: Christian Literature, 1895). Revised and edited by Kevin Knight. https://www.newadvent.org/fathers/3601.htm.
Griffin, William, et al. "Contemporary Apostles and the Pentecostal Assemblies of Canada." PAOC, Nov. 2002. Position Paper. https://paoc.org/docs/default-source/church-toolbox/position-papers/contemporary-apostles/contemporary-apostles-2022.pdf?sfvrsn=d97df36a_4.
Griffith, Susannah. *Forgiveness After Trauma: A Path to Find Healing and Empowerment*. Grand Rapids: Brazos, 2024.
Guest, Mathew. *Neoliberal Religion: Faith and Power in the Twenty-First Century*. New York: Bloomsbury Academic, 2022.
Hastings, W. Ross. *Pastoral Ethics: Moral Formation as Life in the Trinity*. Bellingham, WA: Lexham Academic, 2022.
Hazzard, David, et al. "Contemporary Prophets and Prophecy." PAOC, Nov. 2007. Position Paper. https://paoc.org/docs/default-source/church-toolbox/position-papers/contemporary-prophets-prophecy/contemporary-prophets-and-prophecy.pdf?sfvrsn=f06e196a_2.
Hildebrandt, Lillian Barbara. "Curriculum Development for Worship in the Pentecostal Assemblies of Canada." DEd diss., University of South Africa, 2008. http://hdl.handle.net/10500/1945.

Bibliography

Imes, Carmen Joy. *Bearing God's Name: Why Sinai Still Matters.* Downers Grove, IL: IVP Academic, 2019.

Indeed Employer Content Team. "Ontario Overtime Pay vs Other Provinces in Canada." Indeed for Employers, last updated Jan. 8, 2025. https://ca.indeed.com/hire/c/info/overtime-pay-ontario-other-provinces.

Johnson, Van, et al., eds. *Essential Truths: The PAOC Statement of Essential Truths; Commentary.* Pentecostal Assemblies of Canada International Office, 2023. https://dq5pwpg1q8ruo.cloudfront.net/2023/03/21/13/00/43/12789424-69c0-4ae8-88a5-5abbf87ccf7b/Essential%20Truths%20-%20PAOC-2023.pdf.

Jones, Princess. "Hulu Series Shows the Gravity of Hillsong's High and Low Notes." Religion Unplugged, May 31, 2023. https://religionunplugged.com/news/2023/5/31/hulu-series-shows-the-gravity-of-hillsong-churchs-hubristic-highs-and-lows.

Kant, Immanuel. *Lectures on Ethics.* Edited by J. B. Schneewind. Translated by Peter Heath. Cambridge Edition of the Works of Immanuel Kant. Cambridge: Cambridge University Press, 2001.

Langberg, Diane. *Redeeming Power: Understanding Authority and Abuse in the Church.* Grand Rapids: Brazos, 2020.

Lee, Stacey, dir. *The Secrets of Hillsong.* Season 1, Episode 4, "False Prophets." Aired May 26, 2023, on FX. https://www.hulu.com/series/the-secrets-of-hillsong-41cb2b50-df48-485c-8963-0aafca4a8601.

Liu, Lisha. "Using Generic Inductive Approach in Qualitative Educational Research: A Case Study Analysis." *Journal of Education and Learning* 5 (2016) 129–35.

Luscombe, Jason. "Here to Serve: Reclaiming a Sense of Urgency to the Call of God." *Testimony/Enrich*, Summer 2023. https://testimony.paoc.org/articles/here-to-serve.

McKnight, Scot. *A Community Called Atonement.* Living Theology. Nashville: Abingdon, 2007.

Mehta, Shikha. "What Are the Overtime Rules in Canada?" Canadian Payroll Services, Dec. 17, 2024. https://canadianpayrollservices.com/overtime-rules-canada/.

Moltmann-Wendel, Elizabeth, and Jürgen Moltmann. "To Believe with All Your Senses: The Resurrection of the Body." *Proceedings of the Catholic Theological Society of America* 60 (2006) 1–12.

Mullen, Wade. *Something's Not Right: Decoding the Hidden Tactics of Abuse and Freeing Yourself from Its Power.* Carol Stream, IL: Tyndale Momentum, 2020.

Nadon, Sarah. "Test for Breach of Confidence." *Carson Law*, Sept. 1, 2020. Edited by Ryan Carson. https://www.carsonlaw.ca/ourblog/breachofconfidence.

Niebuhr, Helmut Richard. *The Responsible Self: An Essay in Christian Moral Philosophy.* New York: Harper & Row, 1978.

Nye, Joseph S. "The Changing Nature of Power." In *Soft Power: The Means To Success In World Politics.* New York: PublicAffairs, 2009. Kindle.

BIBLIOGRAPHY

OCASI [Ontario Council of Agencies Serving Immigrants]. "Where Can I Get Information About Regulated Professions?" Settlement, last updated July 25, 2023. https://settlement.org/ontario/employment/professions-and-trades/regulated/where-can-i-find-career-maps-for-trades-and-regulated-professions/.

Ogden, Steven G. *The Church, Authority, and Foucault: Imagining the Church as an Open Space of Freedom*. Routledge New Critical Thinking in Religion, Theology, and Biblical Studies. London: Routledge, Taylor & Francis, 2017.

Ontario. "Employment Standards Act, 2000, S.O. 2000, c. 41." Ontario, 2000. https://www.ontario.ca/laws/statute/00e41.

Ontario Human Rights Commission. *Minds That Matter: Report on the Consultation on Human Rights, Mental Health and Addictions*. Ontario Human Rights Commission, 2012. https://www3.ohrc.on.ca/sites/default/files/Minds%20that%20matter_Report%20on%20the%20consultation%20on%20human%20rights%2C%20mental%20health%20and%20addictions.pdf.

Pellowe, John. "How Christian Is My Ministry?" Christian Leadership Reflections, Apr. 2, 2010. https://www.cccc.org/news_blogs/john/2010/04/02/how-christian-is-my-ministry/.

Penrod, Janice, et al. "A Discussion of Chain Referral as a Method of Sampling Hard-to-Reach Populations." *Journal of Transcultural Nursing* 14 (2003) 100–107.

Pentecostal Assemblies of Canada, The. "2022 Fellowship Statistics." PAOC, Jan. 18, 2023. https://web.archive.org/web/20231021131420/https://paoc.org/docs/default-source/fellowship-services-documents/fellowship-stats-2022-at-18-jan-2023-final.pdf.

———. "2023 National Leadership Conference and Annual General Meeting." PAOC, 2023. https://paoc.org/events/annual-general-meeting-2023.

———. "55th General Conference, May 17–18, 2022: Minutes." PAOC, 2022. https://paoc.org/docs/default-source/events/gc2022/minutes/gc-2022-minutes.pdf?sfvrsn=5fbef16a_6.

———. "General Constitution and By-Laws, 2022: By-Law 10." PAOC, 2022. https://paoc.org/docs/default-source/fellowship-services-documents/constitutions/2022-constitutions-updated/general-constitution-and-by-laws_by-law10.pdf?sfvrsn=d26cfb6a_4.

———. "Ministerial Code of Ethics." PAOC, n.d. https://paoc.org/docs/default-source/fellowship-services-documents/ministerial-code-of-ethics.pdf?sfvrsn=fa351d6a_2.

———. "PAOC Statement of Affirmation Regarding the Equality of Women and Men in Leadership." PAOC, June 2018. https://paoc.org/docs/default-source/church-toolbox/position-papers/statements/paoc-statement-of-affirmation-regarding-the-equality-of-women-and-men-in-leadership.pdf?sfvrsn=ce4ce26a_12.

———. *Personnel Policies, Procedures & Practices Manual for [Name of Church]* [titled in link as *Customizable Personnel Manual for Church Admin*

BIBLIOGRAPHY

Manual]. PAOC, Jan. 2016. From *ABNWT District Church Administration Manual*. https://web.archive.org/web/20210509081814/https://paoc.org/ministry-toolbox/church-resource-documents/church-administration/tab-details.

———. "Special Meeting of the General Conference of the Pentecostal Assemblies of Canada (Calvary Temple, Winnipeg, Manitoba): Minutes." PAOC, Apr. 21, 2022. https://paoc.org/docs/default-source/events/gc2022/special-meeting-minutes/minutes---2022-special-meeting-of-the-general-conference.pdf?sfvrsn=f543f06a_4.

Pittman, Holly. "Seals and Sealings in the Sumerian World." In *The Sumerian World*, edited by Harriet Crawford, 319–42. Routledge Worlds. London: Routledge, 2016.

Poirier, Albert. *The Peacemaking Pastor*. Grand Rapids: Baker, 2006.

Poling, James N. *The Abuse of Power: A Theological Problem*. Nashville: Abingdon, 1991.

Presbyterian Church in Canada, The. "Continuing Education Regulations." Presbyterian Church in Canada, Mar. 2012. https://web.archive.org/web/20220420011909/https://presbyterian.ca/wp-content/uploads/mcv_continuing_education_regulations_2012-03-16.pdf.

Provan, Iain. *Seriously Dangerous Religion: What the Old Testament Really Says and Why It Matters*. Waco: Baylor University Press, 2014.

Provan, Iain, et al. *A Biblical History of Israel*. Louisville: Westminster John Knox, 2003.

Richard, James, et al. "Miracles and Healings." PAOC, Nov. 2007. Position Paper. https://paoc.org/docs/default-source/church-toolbox/position-papers/miracles-healing/miracles-and-healing.pdf?sfvrsn=8f6e196a_2.

Riis, Thomas. "Analysis of Working Hours." *Diogenes* 38 (1990) 65–83.

Royal Canadian Mounted Police. "Become a Police Officer with Federal Policing: Undergo Medical and Psychological Assessments." RCMP Careers, last modified Aug. 20, 2024. https://rcmp.ca/en/careers/become-police-officer-with-federal-policing-undergo-medical-psychological-assessments.

Roys, Julie. "James MacDonald Is Fired: A Day to Mourn, to Pray, & to Plead for Revival." *Roys Report*, Feb. 13, 2019. https://julieroys.com/james-macdonald-fired-day-mourn-pray-plead-revival/.

Russell, Kenneth. "Choosing God's Call over Your Career." BC and Yukon District of the Pentecostal Assemblies of Canada, Jan. 30, 2024. https://bcyd.ca/choosing-gods-call-over-your-career-obeying-god-unconditionally/.

Sasha, Joy. "'The Secrets of Hillsong': The 8 Major Bombshells from FX's New Hillsong Church Docuseries." *Salon*, May 27, 2023. https://www.salon.com/2023/05/27/the-secrets-of-hillsong-the-8-major-bombshells-from-fxs-new-hillsong-church-docuseries/.

Schwarz, Hans. "Human Destiny." In *The Human Being: A Theological Anthropology*, 343–57. Grand Rapids: Eerdmans, 2013.

BIBLIOGRAPHY

Service Canada. *Employment Insurance and Fraud*. Service Canada, 2018. EDSC Cat. No. IN-215-02-18E. https://www.canada.ca/content/dam/canada/employment-social-development/programs/ei/ei-list/reports/fraud-serious/EI-and-fraud-EN.pdf.

Seward, Karen. *Balancing Workplace Mental Health Issues and Employee Privacy Rights*. Cira, 2013. https://cirahealth.ca/assets/docs/WP-Resource-BalancingWorkplaceMentalHealthandPrivacy-EN.pdf.

Shechter, Olga G., and Eric L. Lang. *Identifying Personality Disorders That Are Security Risks: Field Test Results*. Defense Technical Information Center, Sept. 2011. Technical Report 11-05. https://apps.dtic.mil/sti/citations/ADA564011.

Shelley, Bruce L. "Splitting Important Hairs: The Doctrine of the Trinity." In *Church History in Plain Language*, edited by Marshall Shelley, 127–37. 5th ed. Grand Rapids: Zondervan Academic, 2020.

Social Concerns Committee. "Dignity of Human Life." PAOC, Nov. 7, 2001. Poisiton Paper. https://www.paoc.org/docs/default-source/church-toolbox/position-papers/dignity-of-human-life/dignity-of-human-life.pdf?sfvrsn=db6e196a_2.

Stankorb, Sarah. *Disobedient Women: How a Small Group of Faithful Women Exposed Abuse, Brought Down Powerful Pastors, and Ignited an Evangelical Reckoning*. Franklin, TN: Worthy, 2024.

Steed, Chris. *Smart Leadership—Wise Leadership: Environments of Value in an Emerging Future*. New York: Routledge, Taylor & Francis, 2017.

Study Commission. "A Biblical and Theological Study of Authority." PAOC, Nov. 2010. https://paoc.org/docs/default-source/church-toolbox/position-papers/authority/authority.pdf?sfvrsn=586f196a_2.

Swinton, John, and Harriet Mowat. *Practical Theology and Qualitative Research*. London: SCM, 2006.

Sykes, Stephen. *Power and Christian Theology*. New York: Continuum, 2006.

Synan, Vinson, ed. *The Century of the Holy Spirit: 100 Years of Pentecostal and Charismatic Renewal, 1901–2001*. Nashville: Thomas Nelson, 2001.

Taylor, Derrick Bryson. "Carl Lentz, Pastor to Celebrities, Is Fired from Hillsong Church." *New York Times*, Nov. 5, 2020; updated Aug. 5, 2021. https://www.nytimes.com/2020/11/05/us/hillsong-carl-lentz-fired.html.

Thomas, David R. "A General Inductive Approach for Analyzing Qualitative Evaluation Data." *American Journal of Evaluation* 27 (2006) 237–46.

Tran, Jonathan. "Part 1: Power and Totality." In *Foucault and Theology*, 15–124. Philosophy and Theology. New York: T&T Clark, 2011.

Trask, Thomas E., et al., eds. *The Pentecostal Pastor*. Springfield, MO: Gospel, 1997.

Uyen, Vu. "Top Court Sets Limits on Duty to Accommodate." *HR Reporter*, Aug. 11, 2008. https://www.hrreporter.com/focus-areas/employment-law/top-court-sets-limits-on-duty-to-accommodate/288138.

Van Kleef, Gerben A., et al. "Power, Distress, and Compassion: Turning a Blind Eye to the Suffering of Others." *Psychological Science* 19 (2008) 1315–22.

Bibliography

Watkins, Clare. *Disclosing Church: An Ecclesiology Learned from Conversations in Practice*. London: Routledge, 2020.

Watts, Fraser, et al. "Clergy." In *Psychology for Christian Ministry*, 250–64. London: Routledge, 2002.

———. "Social Processes in Church Life." In *Psychology for Christian Ministry*, 207–23 .London: Routledge, 2002.

———. "The Church as an Organisation." In *Psychology for Christian Ministry*, 224–49. London: Routledge, 2002.

———. "Unhealthy Religion." In *Psychology for Christian Ministry*, 59–75. London: Routledge, 2002.

Watts, Rikk E. *The Gospel of Mark: A Commentary on His Use of the Old Testament*. Vancouver: Regent College Publishing, 2017.

Wells, David. "Aligned for Mission." *Testimony*, Winter 2023. https://www.digitaltestimonymag.ca/testimony/winter_2023/MobilePagedArticle.action?articleId=1851228#articleId1851228/.

———. "A Culture of Honour." *Testimony/Enrich*, Spring 2023. https://paoc.org/mission-global/global-view/2023/05/08/a-culture-of-honour/.

———. "What We Call Ourselves." *Testimony/Enrich*, Summer 2020. https://paoc.org/mission-global/global-view/2020/07/29/what-we-call-ourselves/.

Wilkinson, Michael, and Linda McGuire Ambrose. *After the Revival: Pentecostalism and the Making of a Canadian Church*. Montreal: McGill-Queen's University Press, 2020.

www.ingramcontent.com/pod-product-compliance
Lightning Source LLC
Chambersburg PA
CBHW060821190426
43197CB00038B/2177